PORNOGRAPHY
SEX
AND
FEMINISM

■

Also by Alan Soble

Pornography: Marxism, Feminism, and the Future of Sexuality

The Structure of Love

Sexual Investigations

The Philosophy of Sex and Love: An Introduction

[ed.] *The Philosophy of Sex: Contemporary Readings*

[ed.] *Eros, Agape, and Philia: Readings in the Philosophy of Love*

[ed.] *Sex, Love, and Friendship*

PORNOGRAPHY
SEX
AND
FEMINISM

■

ALAN SOBLE

 **Prometheus Books**

59 John Glenn Drive
Amherst, New York 14228-2197

Published 2002 by Prometheus Books

Inquiries should be addressed to
Prometheus Books
59 John Glenn Drive
Amherst, New York 14228–2197
VOICE: 716–691–0133, ext. 207
FAX: 716–564–2711
WWW.PROMETHEUSBOOKS.COM

06 05 04 03 02   5 4 3 2 1

Library of Congress Cataloging-in-Publication Data

Soble, Alan.
    Pornography, sex, and feminism / Alan Soble.
       p. cm.
    Includes bibliographical references and index.
    ISBN 1–57392–944–1 (alk. paper)
    1. Pornography. 2. Feminism. 3. Conservatism. I. Title.

HQ471 .S635 2002
363.4'7—dc21   2002019176

Printed in Canada on acid-free paper

For Rachel Emőke

CONTENTS

PREFACE

I have written before on pornography, human sexuality, and feminism, including scholarly essays published in the journals *Social Theory and Practice* (1985) and *Social Epistemology* (1988); my first monograph, *Pornography: Marxism, Feminism, and the Future of Sexuality* (1986); and chapter six of my *Sexual Investigations* (1996). Over that ten-year period, I found my perspective on the world and its inhabitants, my views about particular philosophical and social issues, and my style of expressing or communicating my thoughts changing. All these—my beliefs, my analyses, and my language—became less formulaic and casuistic, providing me with a surprising and welcome sense of freedom, and—I perceive no way of avoiding or sweetening such a crude confession—they seemed as well to come closer to the truth. The evolution of my general philosophical take on existence, of the nature of the positions I am inclined to defend and dispute, and of the way in which I feel comfortable sharing my thoughts with others, has continued. *Pornography, Sex, and Feminism* is the pungent product (perhaps in the tart style, but hardly the monodimensional substance, of the antipornography feminist Catharine MacKinnon) of that continued evolution. Who knows what the new millennium, let alone the final decade of my professional career, will bring.

Small portions of *Pornography, Sex, and Feminism* were taken from "Disorder and Diversity," my keynote address for the University of New Orleans colloquium "Towards 2000: Gender Diversity Now and into the Next Century," which I delivered orally on Friday, April 18, 1997. I thank the organizers of the colloquium for that exciting and enjoyable opportunity and for the stipend. Other small portions were lifted from my remarks delivered orally at a meeting of the Philosophers for Social Responsibility, held during the Central Division meetings of the American Philosophical Association in Chicago, April 1987. (The meeting was devoted to a discussion of my 1986 book *Pornography*.) The full written texts that served as the foundations for these two oral lectures can be found on my home page, the URL of which is http://www.uno.edu/~asoble; on this page, click on the link "Published Essays, Books, and Other Stuff" and scroll down. A couple of small passages have been taken from *Pornography* (now out of print and occasionally stolen from libraries), and I borrowed a footnote from my essay "Bad Apples: Feminist Politics and Feminist Scholarship"; these materials have been rewritten and developed to fit into the context of the points I make in *Pornography, Sex, and Feminism*.

I thank Jennifer Poché, Lesley Jane, Lisa Z. Sigel, Martha Cornog, Tim Perper, Jim Stone, Jessica Munns, Jerry Nosich, Patrick Hopkins, I. C. Jarvie, Kathrin Koslicki, Jennifer Sumner, Patricia Petersen, Richard Hull, Keith Burgess-Jackson, Edward Johnson, Anastasia Rey, Kathleen Flick, Antoinette Marino, Della Gonzales, Peggy Brinkman, Meghann French, and Mom and Dad for their valuable help. I am sure that other people, both friends and colleagues, helped during the book's composition (1998–2001); I am sorry not to be able to name them. Most important was the constitutional cheerfulness and energy of my daughter, Rachel, and her nagging insistence on getting a *csemege* (a treat), which kept me quite happy while writing this small book. Eventually, we shall learn whether she appreciates that this book and *Sexual Investigations* have been dedicated to her—indeed, whether she takes any interest at all in her old daddy's confounding writings on sexuality.

ONE

MEANING, DIVERSITY, POLYSEMICITY

Tolerance is the solution liberalism offers. A very substantive sexual blackmail lies at the heart of this liberal tolerance. In order not to criticize anyone's sexuality, it is women, specifically, who are used and abused by men, women who are sacrificed. . . . [T]he defense of lesbian sadomasochism would sacrifice all women's ability to walk down the street in safety for the freedom to torture a woman in the privacy of one's basement . . . in the name of everyone's freedom of choice.
Catharine MacKinnon, *Feminism Unmodified* (p. 15)

BRUTALITY

Antipornography feminists are fond of pointing out—better, merely asserting—that a common theme of pornography is the mutilation of women. Consider the accusation voiced by Margaret Baldwin, then a law student who studied under Catharine MacKinnon:

In pornography, the world is a balanced and harmonious place. The sexual requirements of women and men are perfectly congruent, symbiotic in relation and polar in definition: women live to be fucked, men inevitably fuck. Women especially love to be fucked by animals, dildoes, fists, and penises, especially while being bound, beaten, cut, mutilated and killed. . . . Men inevitably fuck. Fortunately for us, they love to fuck us in all the ways we love to be fucked. This is the version of sexual equality that is in the mouths of the pornographers who tell us they love women.[1]

Where is all this horrible stuff? The usenet newsgroup alt.binaries.pictures.erotica.rape is merely one of many hundreds of pornographic newsgroups on the Internet, and the photographs it makes available are tame, as are the images on the newsgroup alt.binaries.pictures.erotica.bondage. One thing Baldwin says is correct. Pornography displays some sort of sexual equality or utopian (for her, dystopian) congruity in the sexual natures of men and women. But men do not "inevitably" fuck in pornography, or engage in "ramming up," in Catharine MacKinnon's caustic language.[2] Far from it; have a look at the overwhelming variety of fuckless pornography displayed on the Internet. Nor is violent and mutilating sexuality as common in pornography as Baldwin implies. In a note, Baldwin says that "authority for this synopsis was gleaned from pornography readily available at this time in Minneapolis."[3] Six of her sixteen exhibits are from *Hustler*, which enjoys deliberately offending Baldwinians and others having tender sensibilities. Another "exhibit" is her reference to the notorious but apocryphal snuff film. Baldwin's examples (*Hustler*, the snuff film) are skewed. Further, she homogenizes and stereotypes pornography instead of paying attention to its variety; she does not "listen" to the organism.[4] Baldwin's accusation is frequently repeated by people who, it seems, have little acquaintance with pornography. "If pornography does help create a dangerous social climate, the most irresponsible pornography would be that picturing women being violently abused. Some pornography pictures women being beaten, raped, held in bondage, and even murdered. This is degrading and dehumanizing, especially when women are pictured as willing victims," claims Don Marietta, providing no evidence that women have been murdered (willingly?) in the making of pornography.[5] MacKinnon, too—a professor of law at the University of Michigan, who ought to know better about how properly to make claims and support them with evidence—makes the bombastic and flimsy accusation that women are murdered for and in pornography.[6] Such antipornography arguments engage in suspicious overkill, premised on ignorance of the genre or malicious misrepresentation.

For example: Marty Rimm reports, in his Carnegie Mellon study of pornography available on the Internet, that when images of women performing fellatio on men are advertised and described as "choking" images by their sellers, consumers download these images twice as often as they download fellatio images advertised and described merely as, for example, "sucking cock" images.[7] Rimm does *not* report that there is *any* difference in the content of these images differently described; he does not claim that in the images described as "choking," the man's penis enters more deeply or more violently into the woman's mouth, or that it goes into her throat. (In attempting to entice consumers to make purchases, overzealous sellers of images overdescribe their wares the same way that overzealous feminist and conservative critics of pornography, to condemn the genre, overdescribe its content—perhaps, in effect, also enticing people to take a look.) Yet consider MacKinnon's summary of what Rimm found:

> When a woman is marketed being intensely physically harmed, consumer demand doubles; fellatio gets a lukewarm response, but downloads double for "choking." . . . The Carnegie Mellon study disproves allegations that those who oppose the pornography industry have distorted its largely benign reality.[8]

This is both misleading and incomplete. At the very least, MacKinnon should have indicated that she and Rimm are speaking only about written descriptions of images (an advertising framing device), and not their pictorial content, by putting the word *fellatio* (better, "sucking cock") between quotation marks, as she does for *choking*. MacKinnon here emphasizes the brutality of pornographic images by smearing the difference between description and content; her conclusion in the passage, which depends on there being actual choking or other physical harm in the images, does not follow. Furthermore, MacKinnon's use of the word *lukewarm* in describing consumer response to "sucking cock" advertisements of fellatio images is an overstatement, given Rimm's data; and her argument that downloads double in response to a "choking" description vindicates her view of the brutality of pornographic images also ignores Rimm's data. For, according to Rimm, on the particular bulletin board system (BBS) from which he gathered his information on this topic, only 2.4 percent of the downloads were of "sucking cock" images,[9] which is in my book not a "lukewarm" response, but nearly a sign of complete disinterest. The doubling, then, was only to 4.8 percent, a magnificently low figure that no one would ever have guessed from MacKinnon's rendition of Rimm's study, and not a convincing sign of the brutality of pornography or of men in general as consumers. Why didn't MacKinnon mention the crucial statistic that downloads of images described as "choking" were under 5 percent?— because doing so would show that her accusations against pornography were nothing but hot air. This is just one of many examples of MacKinnon's sloppy, or deliberately ambiguous, writing. It helps explain why some people, with some justification, accuse her and other antipornography feminists of exaggerating the extent of brutality in pornography and in the sexual psychology of men.

According to MacKinnon's dismal, even paranoid, view of the sexuality of men, "hostility," "hatred," and "death" provoke the "penis [to] shudder and stiffen."[10] "Men masturbate," she says scornfully, "to women being exposed, humiliated, violated, degraded, mutilated, dismembered, bound, gagged, tortured, and killed."[11] MacKinnon says these inflammatory things about men and their sexuality, as does Andrea Dworkin (men need pornography because "men love death"),[12] but she really doesn't know them to be true. This distorted view of the psychology of men follows from MacKinnon's equally distorted view of the content of pornography and her simplistic methodology:

> Thus the question Freud never asked is the question that defines sexuality in a feminist perspective: what do men want? Pornography provides an answer. . . . It shows what men want and gives it to them. From the testimony of pornography, what men want is: women bound, women battered, women tortured, women humiliated, women degraded and defiled, women killed.[13]

"What men want"—what *all* men want—is MacKinnon's silly generalization. With astonishing dogmatic confidence, MacKinnon concludes that "[t]he message of these materials . . . is 'get her,' pointing at all women. . . . This message is addressed directly to the penis, delivered through an erection, and taken out on women in the real world."[14] For MacKinnon, men do not exist. Only the penis exists. And the penis is the man's brain; it does all his thinking. MacKinnon does to men what she believes men and pornography do to women, that is, reduce them to the status of their genitals, to the status of pure sex item and object.[15]

How to Study Pornography

MacKinnon's methodology of drawing grandiose conclusions about men and their sexuality on the basis of the surface content of (some) pornography is also embraced by Andrea Dworkin's companion, John Stoltenberg. For him, pornography is "a window into acculturated male sexuality"; it "is about the most reliable evidence that we have about male sexual identity"; and it "tells lies about women [but] tells the truth about men."[16] MacKinnon and Stoltenberg assume a literal match between pornographic portrayals and what is in the minds of men or what men find sexually arousing. Or maybe they are right in principle (even if unsubtle in the application), that the content of men's minds and their sexual interests can somehow be inferred from the content of pornography; nevertheless, they have a distorted view of the content of pornography. What, for Stoltenberg, is the truth that pornography tells about men? Pornography "reveals . . . an addiction to force and coercion for arousal, eroticized racial hatred, a despisal of the female, a fetishizing of erection and devotion to penetration, . . . [and] an eroticized commitment to violence."[17] This is another false, perhaps intentionally so, statement about men and pornography. To be charitable (based on my reading of their work), neither MacKinnon nor Stoltenberg know the content of pornography or how to read it. As the film critic and scholar Linda Williams, who immersed herself in pornography in order to write a book about it, observes: "[T]o my surprise, in the genre where I expected to see the most unrelieved and unchallenged dominance of the phallus (literally, in the form of the ubiquitous erect or ejaculating penis), I saw instead a remarkable uncertainty and instability."[18]

There are, then, two points to be made against analyses of pornography like those of MacKinnon and Stoltenberg.[19]

First, the content of pornography is not monolithic; the diversity of pornographic images, apparent to anyone who studies the material with attentive care, is astounding. This multiplicity undercuts the attempt to tease out one dominant message from pornography, including the notion that pornography disseminates brazen, "get her," mutilating misogyny. Consider, as one alternative to this stock unmodified feminist reading, the suggestion that in pornography

> we find a male popular culture that . . . neither disregards nor blames the woman in its attempt to renegotiate the sexual and social status quo, a male popular culture that devotes itself . . . to examining the hearts of men. What's in the hearts of men according to porn? A utopian desire for a world where women aren't socially required to say and believe that they don't like sex as much as men do.[20]

This is a neat alternative or supplement to MacKinnon's "get her" reading of pornography, but if there is a single message that can be extracted from all pornography, from all the different kinds of pornography, it would have to be a more general message: Heterosexual men as a group, not necessarily individually, enjoy everything sexual, if it is associated pictorially (or in reality) with a young, firm, pretty female face and body, or even an occasional old or flabby body; and homosexual men are similarly indiscriminate or catholic in their tastes. The only general message derivable from the content of pornography borders on being a tautology.

Second, the meaning of the content of various pornographies cannot be read straight off from the surface content of the images; the images are more complex than the critics of pornography allow, especially when we take into account what the images mean to those who consume them for purposes of sexual arousal and sexual pleasure. The intrusion of the wishes, fears, and values of the viewer into the viewing experience—a factor that literalist readers of pornography either ignore or are simply not able to fathom—colors or changes the surface content in idiosyncratic ways. The failure of the critics of pornography to attempt to read pornographic images from the perspective of individual viewers (to see the images as the men see them), or to attempt genuinely to understand the minds and hearts of the mostly male consumers of pornography, is a moral failure of empathetic identification, and it leads the critics of pornography to misrepresent and misconstrue pornographic images. Not viewing pornographic images from the perspective of their users, the critics, both feminist and conservative, fill in the resulting epistemic vacuum with their own worst nightmares.

To convince yourself of the variety of pornography, browse the sexual usenet newsgroups (America Online provides connections to over five hundred). Newsgroups supply free pornography—a boon to the researcher, who thereby avoids the fees of Web sites that charge for visiting, viewing, and downloading (many of the "http:" sex sites on the Internet, as well as the bulletin board systems). Much, often most, of the pornography available in the newsgroups is prepared, sorted, and posted by users for users, sometimes with helpful thumbnail indices* (but watch out for annoying commercial spam).[21] Examine these newsgroups (type "news:" before the URL if you are accessing these sites from AOL; otherwise, the usenet newsgroup protocol is "nntp:"):

- alt.binaries.pictures.erotica.orientals (high-quality scans of Asian women; some hard-core; some solo Asian males)

---

*For a nonpornographic example of the use of thumbnails, go to www.uno.edu/~asoble/pages/rart.htm.

- alt.binaries.fetish.scat (women defecating alone or on men or women; solo males defecating; men dumping on women)
- alt.binaries.pictures.erotica.oral (some men *do* like fellatio; also photographs of solo men displaying their penises)
- alt.pantyhose (women, and some men, posing in pantyhose)
- alt.binaries.pictures.erotica.female.anal (women receiving anal intercourse)
- alt.sex.femdom (men spanked, whipped, bound, dildoed, humiliated, and ruled by women)
- alt.binaries.pictures.erotica.panties (undergarments of all colors and styles, worn by women—and men—of all colors and styles)
- alt.smokers.glamour (fully dressed, nude, or partially nude women smoking cigarettes or, sometimes, cigars)
- alt.binaries.pictures.erotica.close-up (genitals right in your face)
- alt.binaries.erotica.fetish (a mixed bag of enterprising fetishes)
- alt.binaries.pictures.erotica.bondage (women bound in various poses; there are usually no men in the photographs and very little sexual intercourse or fellatio; plenty of female domination of men mixed in)
- alt.binaries.pictures.erotica.transvestites (professional models and amateurs posing partially nude or nude and engaging in sexual activity)
- alt.sex.fetish.feet (toes, heels, soles, nail polish; hard and soft penises grabbed between feet)
- alt.binaries.pictures.erotica.tasteless (tampons and menstruation, bestiality, dildos, gynecological examinations, vomiting, etc.)
- alt.binaries.nospam.female.bodyhair (shows women's

armpit, genital, anal, and leg hair, in contrast to news-groups containing photographs of women who are cleanly shaved genitally or all over)

- alt.binaries.pictures.erotica.male.anal (men giving and getting anal intercourse and fellatio)
- alt.binaries.spanking and alt.binaries.pictures.erotica. spanking (everyone gets it good from everyone else: m/m, m/f, f/f, and f/m spankings)
- alt.binaries.pictures.fetish.latex (women posing in latex, spandex, lycra, rubber, and leather)
- alt.binaries.great.ass.paulina (women showing their rears and anuses)
- alt.binaries.pictures.bigbutts (photographs of big women, both Caucasian and Negro, displaying large, often enormous, asses, nude or tightly clothed)
- alt.binaries.pictures.erotica.high-heels (of which there are more kinds than I had ever imagined)
- alt.binaries.pictures.erotica.latinas (or filipinas or blacks or brunettes or lesbians or . . .)
- alt.binaries.pictures.erotica.torture (equal opportunity victimization, with breast bondage mixed together with cock and ball torture).

And, of course, alt.binaries.pictures.erotica.rape. Some of the descriptions or captions of the photographs in this news-group of heterosexual intercourse and fellatio say "rape," but—MacKinnon would not scoff at this[22]—the sex acts look like ordinary, even dull, sex. The description "rape," like the description "incest," can be attached at will to any photo-graph at all and has no power to make the content of the pho-tograph correspond to what it says it is. Describing a photo-graph as "rape" or "incest" may just be another marketing gimmick.

Women scholars who want to study and write about

pornography no longer have the excuse, for not looking at much of it, that doing a proper survey requires that they make a vulnerable spectacle of themselves by grazing in that ugly, dirty, smelly male domain, the demeaned and demeaning United States pornography store.[23] Women scholars now have the Internet, and they can sit safely at home and lurk sex sites with their coffee, cigarette, candy, or clitoris in hand.[24] Note that many pornographic newsgroups focus on a single sexual activity or sexual interest to which they cater ("market segmentation"), and that their topics, in many cases, are paraphilias or (according to the ordinary understanding of these matters) kinks or sexual perversions. Thus it could be argued that the newsgroups—by being pluralistic, democratic, and anonymous—provide an unprecedented source of sexual stimulation and affirmation for those people, largely men, who have "minority," even "oppressed," sexual tastes. The Internet is an Alice's Restaurant of pornographic images, and you can get lots of things there other than the vanilla sex of Baldwin's "inevitable fuck" and MacKinnon's "ramming up."

Because there is an abundance of kinky pornography on the Internet (for example, "bestiality and coprophilia images are selling briskly"),[25] Rimm detects an intellectual problem:

> This study suggests a tremendous rift between the sexual activities in which Americans claim to engage, as reported most recently by the study *Sex in America*, and the sexually explicit activities presented in images that many Americans consume.[26]

Rimm seems surprised by this contrast—that Americans report engaging in primarily vanilla sex, yet download millions of fetishistic images from the Internet—and he offers an explanation to resolve the discrepancy or "rift." But I am not surprised by this contrast, although I would be surprised were I to assume (does Rimm implicitly make these assumptions?) either the dubious psychosexual thesis that viewers of pornography largely want to see in pornographic images those sexual events which they already routinely do (as opposed to wanting to see that which they have not had, in reality, much experience doing, or would never think of actually doing), or the equally dubious thesis that there should be a match between the content of the images that viewers download and what they do in their real sexual lives because, in a nutshell, looking at pornographic images of act *A* causes the viewer to do act *A*. Rimm's explanation is simply that the *Sex in America* study[27] and his Carnegie Mellon study tapped into different populations: "[T]he demographics of computer users do not currently mirror those of the general population."[28] What Rimm is proposing, I think, is that in compiling the data for *Sex in America*, the investigators interviewed or surveyed a random sample of ordinary Americans, while Rimm's population consisted of those who lurk on the Internet, and these tend to be the male Perverts of America. I think not. What the contrast reveals is that for the same population of Americans there is a difference between what they do sexually, or what they feel comfortable telling strangers they do sexually, and what their deepest and perhaps most embarrassing fantasies are, fantasies that they can indulge only through pornography and, now, without much difficulty, by accessing appropriate images on the Internet. The contrast also reveals, I think, the gap between male and female sexuality, or between the sexuality of men and that of women: Male or men's sexuality is more variable, taking delight not only in heterosexual coitus but in the whole range of sexual possibilities. Men, perverts one and all, have found their home on the Internet.

MESSAGES

Based on the "testimony" of pornography, that sexual images come in all sorts of styles and not very much of it is brutal, pornography's message is not MacKinnon's "get her." It is closer to "worship her," in all her endless variety. But not even the postmodernist woman scholar Berkeley Kaite, who does not take the unmodified feminist view of pornography and who claims to find a specific, even if by now hackneyed message in its pictorial richness—namely, almost everything in pornography signifies the phallus:[29] the female breast, a high-heeled shoe—did not do her observatory homework. Consider these assertions about the content of pornography: (1) "female pornography models are almost never completely naked"[30] (no; the models are often, if not usually, fully naked); (2) the "female model almost never has a bare foot and instead brandishes the stiletto heel"[31] (not even close; Kaite might have focused, if she focused at all, on the high-heels newsgroup); (3) "the single breast is the favored icon (as opposed to both pictured together)"[32] (favored? the single breast is *rare*); (4) in transsexual pornography in which a "straight" male has sex with a shemale, "the male model is never penetrated anally"[33] ("never" is false; these "straight" men also suck plenty of transsexual penis and kiss transsexual ass; see alt.binaries.pictures.erotica.transexual.action); (5) in heterosexual pornography, "the anus is always hers . . . never his"[34] (this is *almost* true for pornography *made* in the United States, in which the male's anus is commonly, but not always, cropped out of pictures of heterosexual couplings; it is certainly false for pornography produced in Europe and Asia, which shows hairy or smooth male anuses during heterosexual intercourse and which is abundantly available on the newsgroups). These are incredible misrepresentations or errors, not a sound basis on which to draw conclusions about

the meaning of pornography and its sexual and psychological appeal to men. Kaite is not a reliable observer or reporter
to begin with: "In Walt Disney animated films, the evil stepmother is often found smoking, an image powerful enough
to signify to very young children."[35] I racked my brain to
find one case of a smoking stepmom in a Disney cartoon,
with the assistance of my daughter, Rachel. We came up with
nothing. There is an evil stepmother in *Cinderella*, but she
doesn't smoke. There is the evil queen in *Snow White*; she
doesn't smoke. Cruella DeVil chain smokes in both versions
of *101 Dalmatians*, but she is no one's stepmother. No wonder
Kaite didn't give any examples.

Noting the diversity of pornographic images, Linda
Williams argues that pornography is "an important means of
representing a wide range of sexual identities once labelled
deviant—gay, lesbian, bisexual, sadomasochistic. . . . [This] has
been remarkably liberating for previously closeted and
repressed sexualities,"[36] including all sorts of paraphiliacs. For
Williams, this defeats MacKinnon's radical pretensions: "To
MacKinnon, pornography is the essence of the power exer-
cised by men over women through sexuality. That pornography could be a form of the sexual speech of heterosexual
women, gays, lesbians and others . . . is to MacKinnon
unthinkable."[37] It is well known that MacKinnon has claimed
that pornography silences women.[38] Given her more accurate
survey of pornographic images, Williams finds that the genre
empowers at least some women and sexual-preference minorities, providing them with valuable modes of speech. Further,
on Williams's view, straight men get off the hook: If "pornography is not the monolithic expression of phallic misogyny that
it has been stigmatised as being, then there is good reason even
for heterosexual men to explore the pleasures of the genre
without having to admit too many *mea culpas*."[39]

Not only does the diversity of pornographic images

undermine the basics of the MacKinnon-Stoltenberg analysis of pornography, but the "polysemicity" of the images, the sensitivity of meaning to the viewer's input, does so as well. Consider a photograph of a woman bending over, exposing her bare bottom. What does *bending over* mean? In itself, nothing. The meaning, the point, of the photograph gets filled in, disambiguated, and defined by the viewer's conscious and unconscious fantasies. When you look at this photograph, do you imagine kissing her ass, or spanking it, or spreading it, or fingering it, or smelling it? Something else? All of it? Even though her ass might be getting spanked, do you imagine, overriding the photograph's surface content, caressing it? Or do you imagine that *you* are getting that spanking or fingering, or that her gorgeous and powerful ass is your gorgeous and powerful ass? Maybe the loving caresses you want to bestow on her rear are the loving caresses you want bestowed on your own rear? Bending over—when it takes the form of mooning a passing passenger train—can also be assertive, aggressive.[40] And, in some cases, the sexual response to an image of bending over might have as much to do with tumbling or hanging breasts, or with the lowering of the face and mouth, or with the accessibility of the genitals, as it does with a spreading or jutting ass. The sexual attraction of bending over might very well be that it is polysemic; viewers might imagine many things at once, tapping in to several unconscious, even contradictory, links at the same time. "Symbols can be as slippery as snakes."[41] Of course, the polysemicity of bending over allows the photograph to express the meaning "get her" (this particular woman, or her ass, not women *simpliciter*), when her ass is seen by the viewer as a target, submissive, something to be spanked or branded or fucked. But, for these images, the meanings "love her" or even "be her" are just as plausible, if not probable, although we have no way to tell, apart from extensive interviews with men instead of dogmatic projections, which meanings predominate. And even such interviews might well be inconclusive. MacKinnon and Stoltenberg studiously pass over the subtleties of images and of sex. As does the *Final Report* (1986) of the Attorney General's [Meese] Commission on Pornography: in describing one image in its many exhibits, the *Final Report* says, "Two close-up photographs of a caucasian female's buttocks spread to expose her anus and vagina."[42] But we cannot tell from the photograph alone what the model meant to expose or what the photographer meant to capture or, especially, what the viewer focuses on when looking at the image. Maybe the model is spreading to expose just her vagina, or just her lips, or just her anus, or just her crack. Maybe the act of spreading is the point, either for her or the viewer. Or she is displaying the strength of her fingers; and so forth. The commission's *Final Report* did not provide us with a brute, uninterpreted description of the image, if in fact one is possible, but gave us only its preferred reading of a polysemic image from all the alternatives.

It is not only a photograph of bending over that is polysemous; the act itself, were it done serendipitously before your very eyes, would also be polysemous: both acts and depictions of acts are polysemous. She bends over, picking up her dropped keys (dropped on purpose?), thereby displaying her ass in tight jeans. Was it purely innocent, or did she do it to arouse you, or to tease you, or to flip you the bird with alternative body language, or did she do it because she is a perverted exhibitionist who likes sticking her ass in the air? You don't know, it happened so quickly and unexpectedly, and perhaps you missed the insult she intended while you were wrapped up in enjoying the sight for its own sake. More important than what is in her mind as she bends over is what is in *your* mind, in particular what is in your mind *about* what is in her mind. You can at will, by entertaining the appropriate fantasy, change her act from an insult to a tease, from "fuck you" to "fuck me." This flexibility applies as much to real-life bendings over as it does to images of bending over. Asking the woman right in front of you, or the model who posed for the photograph, what she meant to do—a potentially disambiguating framing device—might settle the question, but it might not. People lie, or hide their motives, and often do not know their own minds. And if you wanted to, you could continue to read the act or the image the way you prefer to, for your enjoyment, disregarding what was said to you about her intention. United States Supreme Court justices, wrapped up in difficult constitutional matters about the meaning of that document for its original framers, know this quite well.

Other examples of the polysemicity of images are not difficult to provide. Consider a photograph of a woman licking an erect penis, or the act itself. Perhaps she is in control or in charge.[43] She is responsible for his pleasure, she can stop inconsiderately, or nibble the wrong way or cause distraction, or break the spell by coughing or pausing to pick a pubic hair out of her mouth. She has the choice and the power to prolong or end his pleasure. He is grateful for what he receives. Or perhaps he is in control, taking all the pleasure he can get from her lips and tongue, sexually using her submissive mouth as a receptacle. Or they are experimenting: she is curious about the taste and feel of a penis; he is curious about the warmth and wetness of a woman's mouth. Or they are playing boss and secretary, president and intern, or marooned couple on a desert island after a shipwreck. Multiple interpretations of fellatio are possible that are not fixed by the surface content of a depiction or the act, a sexual act that is "fraught with symbolic ambiguity."[44] Is the female fellator a slut, or is she a caring and considerate lover, or is she purely out for her own pleasure? Or suppose a nude woman is bound immobile. She can be perceived as an unwilling (or willing) victim of slavery, as waiting to be sold in an auction to the highest bidder, then to be used sexually by her master. She might be afraid of, or eagerly anticipating, her fate. Or her being bound symbolizes safety, trust, the security of the umbilical cord, a pleasant, temporary escape from the duties of freedom. As the writer Sallie Tisdale confesses, "When I envision my own binding, my submission, I am seeing myself free. Free of guilt, free of responsibility."[45] These readings of bondage pornography and bondage sexual activity are neither mutually exclusive nor exhaustive. A literalist reading of bondage and bondage pornography is possible but shallow.

In some pornographic images, a woman performs an act of fellatio on a photographically isolated penis; the rest of the man is missing or only partially visible. Applied to this type of image, MacKinnon's "get her" reading of pornography, or Dworkin's claim that in pornography "men possess women,"[46] seems to imply that the man is missing so that the viewer can imagine that he is getting the woman, that he is possessing her. But how could the male viewer of this scene imagine that he is the real "possessor" of the woman, or that the missing man's pleasure is his own? That is, of course, possible. But, at the same time, the presence of a penis must remind the viewer that another man *is* there, that the man whose penis is visible is possessing or getting the woman and is experiencing the pleasure, since she is kissing his penis. This *must* undermine the viewer's sense that he is getting her. Perhaps, then, the viewer's pleasure resides in his thinking that at least one fortunate member or representative of the patriarchy is getting her, a representative with whom the viewer can identify as brothers in power. But other readings of this type of pornography are potentially more illuminating. Perhaps the viewer is (un)consciously admiring the penis. Not even he is always aware of the "trigger" in this photograph, which might provoke homosexual desire without much danger by omitting most of the man. The viewer might want to be sucking with gusto what only she, in his mind, is permitted to suck with gusto.[47] So much for the facile classification of pornography that depicts heterosexual acts as "heterosexual" pornography. (Newsgroups primarily devoted to images of women sucking men also contain some images of men sucking men and of solo men displaying their penises.) Maybe the male viewer is primarily aware of the sexual pleasure or arousal he imagines the *woman*, not the man, to be experiencing. Why? In order to increase his own arousal.[48] Perhaps the male viewer "takes the part not of the male, but of the female . . . [and experiences] pleasure in identifying with a 'feminine' passivity or subordination."[49] Hence the fact that the woman is the dramatic and photographic center of the activity, and thereby easy to identify with, while the man is largely absent, merely a spare part. Or the male viewer is aroused because he buys into the social standard according to which women who suck cock, especially those who are paid to do so for photographs, are sluts. But maybe he imagines himself being that slut. What exactly is going on in this interaction between a depiction and the viewer? MacKinnon doesn't know that it means "get her" for him. What it means for the viewer, what registers for him sexually, depends on what he makes with, or adds to, or scrutinizes in, the surface content.

Rimm, without using this terminology, observed that polysemicity attaches to the written descriptions of pornographic images. Considering the description "he watches a hot blonde get fucked," Rimm says that it is not

clear which of the following three keywords were the reason a customer downloaded the image: "watches," "blonde," or "fucked." It would also not be clear whether those three words *in combination* were what especially attracted the customer.[50]

Of course, the attraction might be, for some candidate viewers, none of the words listed by Rimm, but the antici- pated penis of the "he," or the sexiness implied by the "hot," or something else known neither to him nor to us that trig- gers his mouse finger to click into action. Further, if it is not clear what in the description is the enticement, it is also not clear in the pornographic image itself, with its infinity of cues, what brings about the consumer's sexual arousal and pleasure. The principle of polysemicity implies that those who write these finitely brief descriptions must ignore all but a few possible cues in the image; and it is very likely, in their haste to upload and sell, that they do not see much more than a handful of the cues that are in the image. They ignore, for example, that while fucking, this hot blonde's eyes are closed and clenched and that she is caressing the tailbone of her lover. Those customers who would find such details arousing will thus miss their opportunity, if they rely solely on these prepackaged descriptions. In the newsgroups, there is nothing quite as helpful as a thumbnail index that allows the viewer to see all the images quickly, in a smaller version, so that he can pick and choose according to his tastes.

Sadomasochism

The polysemicity of pornographic images and sexual activity has an interesting implication about female-dominant, male- submissive depictions and sexual events. Indeed, it is well to recognize, "By far the most common service paid for by men in heterosexual S/M [sadomasochism] is the extravagant display of [their own] submission. In most commercial B & D [bondage and discipline] ... men are the 'slaves,' not women,"[51] and there is as much female-dominant as there is male-dominant sadomasochistic pornography.[52] The women in female-dominant, male-submissive pornography, and those who engage in this activity commercially, are often delightfully absorbed in what they are doing, relishing their exertion of power over men (a joy that is not gendered, but human). At first sight, female-dominant, male-submissive sadomasochistic pornography and sexual behavior straight-forwardly falsifies, through a literalist reading of their sur-face content, the claim that the message of pornography and the thrust of male sexuality is "get her," since, literally, their meaning is "get him" or "get me." In female-dominant, male-submissive sadomasochism, says the culture and feminist studies professor Anne McClintock, "male 'slaves' enact with compulsive repetition the forbidden knowledge of the power of women."[53] This sadomasochism asserts that women are powerful creatures after all—they are not the wimps they are ordinarily portrayed as being in the mass media—or that, at least, some men (male feminists having a kinky sexual agenda?) wished they were. Feminists, apparently, should welcome female-dominant, male-submissive pornography, if it makes these statements. The "outrage" of female-domi-nant, male-submissive sadomasochistic pornography is that it "publicly exposes the possibility that manhood is not *natu-rally* synonymous with mastery, nor femininity with pas-sivity. ... Men touch each other for pleasure and women wreak well-paid vengeance."[54] Perhaps this is why, according to the anthropologist Carole Vance, "An active edi-torial hand was at work" in the *Final Report* of the Meese Commission "to remove reverse images of female domina-tion and male submission; these images never appeared, though they constitute a significant portion of s/m imagery."[55] On this view, pornography that depicts women dominating men was weeded out by the commission to preserve or protect the commission's preconceived or favored notion that pornography ennobles or glorifies male sexual dominance. Even on a literalist reading of pornography, the Meese Commission, no exemplar of intellectual honesty, unfairly stacked the deck. Did the commission also weed out lesbian sadomasochist pornography to preserve the cultural image of women as always or by their nature nonviolent, caring, gentle, and nurturing? According to the classical historian David Halperin, "Foucault . . . interprets lesbian S/M as the expression of a . . . struggle on the part of women to escape from constraining stereotypes of femininity."[56] That would be a consistent reason for the commission to ignore such depictions. Its *Final Report* does include in its inventory and review of pornographic material titles and descriptions of lesbian (or woman-woman) sadomasochistic pornography,[57] but the commission did not elect to make use of these findings in its discussion of the nature and meaning of contemporary pornography—which fact confirms the spirit, even if not the letter, of Vance's take on the commission's agenda.

But matters are more complex once we go beyond a literalist reading of female-dominant, male-submissive pornography. Linda Williams has observed that

> the male-active-voyeuristic-objectifying side of cinematic spectatorship has been stressed, at the expense of the female-passive-identifying-fetishized . . . side. Even more problematic is the fact that activity and passivity have been too rigorously assigned to separate gendered spectator positions with little examination of either the active elements of the feminine position or the mutability of male and female spectators' adoption of one or the other subject position and participation in the (perverse) pleasures of both.[58]

If a male viewer of female-dominant, male-submissive sado-masochistic pornography identifies not with the supine man who is presenting dorsally or ventrally, but with the erect woman who wears the boot and wields the whip—as a viewer might be identifying, while viewing oral sex images, not with the fellated penis but with the woman who fellates it—then the meaning or point of this image to him is not "get me" but something like "let me, a woman, get him." If so, all bets about the relation between gender and sexual orientation and about the relation between gender and aggression/submission are off. In the use of pornography for sexual arousal and pleasure, whether male-dominant or female-dominant, "identification is mobile, unpredictable, and not bound by either one's actual gender or by practical reality."[59]

Williams's suggestion, based on polysemicity-induced mismatches between the literal content of sadomasochistic images and the meanings that register for its consumers, is that sadomasochistic pornography should be tolerated, encouraged, or applauded because it is the speech of an oppressed sexual minority. (MacKinnon's reply, of sorts, is in the epigraph, above.) This minority has no habit of celebrating or emulating the cruelty and violence of the literal or surface content of sadomasochistic pornography. Practitioners and defenders of sadomasochism have often pointed out, as the feminist writer Gayle Rubin does, that

> SM materials are aimed at an audience that understands a set of conventions for interpreting them. Sadomasochism is not a form of violence, but is rather a type of ritual and contractual sex play whose aficionados go to great lengths . . . to ensure the safety and enjoyment of one another. SM fantasy does involve images of coercion and sexual activities that may appear violent to outsiders. . . . Torn out of context, SM material is upsetting to unprepared audiences.[60]

McClintock elaborates: "Far from being the tyrannical exercise of one will upon a helpless other, consensual S/M is typically collaborative, involving careful training, initiation rites, a scrupulous definition of limits, and a constant confirmation of reciprocity."[61] This is true, apparently, not only of heterosexual sadomasochism, but also of lesbian sadomasochism, which

> constitutes a body of sexual practices in which woman is sexual agent through and through. . . . [T]he masochist acts out her sexuality, constructs scenarios, takes on roles, sets limits. The sadist also acts out her sexuality and takes on roles. . . . Lesbian S/M, then, is a matter of teamwork of female sexual agents. Set in this context, it is hard to read the images of the bound woman simply as a representation of a victim, as a sexual slave, as fetishized object.[62]

Being a matter of teamwork—two considerate people involved in a sadomasochistic sexual session rely on the skills and determination of each other to produce, even maximize, their mutual sexual pleasure—sadomasochism is starting to look like the sexual activity of any other, ordinary, companionate couple. The surface content of sadomasochistic images and behaviors may be violent and brutal, but their underlying meaning is the same old humdrum meaning about values that we have always, by reflex, commended and upheld: care, concern, love.[63] There's not much difference, after all, between rocky road and vanilla. Sadomasochistic pornography, being as polysemous as all pornography is, does not always or often mean what it seems on the surface to mean; nor does sadomasochism itself.

If the principle of polysemicity applies to female-dominant, male-submissive pornography and behavior, and to lesbian sadomasochistic pornography and behavior, then of course it also applies, in particular, and must not be shrugged off, when examining MacKinnon's and Stoltenberg's favorite target: male-dominant, female-submissive sadomasochism. Reading the message "get her" from the surface of hetero-sexual, male-in-charge sadomasochistic pornography is more problematic than MacKinnonites and the commission admit.[64] While looking at this pornography, says the philoso-pher Jean Grimshaw, "the role of the person having the fan-tasy could shift or be quite unclear. . . . [F]antasies commonly offer open, rather than closed, narratives . . . in which the question of identification with the position of victim, agent, voyeur, etc. may be undecidable or shifting."[65] Hence, we should not "assume . . . that if a man watches or fantasises a pornographic scene he is automatically 'identifying' with the man in the picture or the narrative, and desiring to 'do the same.'" Indeed, when viewing male-dominant, female-sub-missive sadomasochistic pornography, "it could be that the subject identifies with the female victim" and does not derive his sexual arousal and pleasure from identifying with the male aggressor.[66]

Grimshaw's claim that the viewer may not desire to "do the same" as the events depicted in the pornographic image may, however, gloss over the crucial point, the point alto-gether missed by Stoltenberg's judging pornography to be "a window into acculturated male sexuality." We can say that the viewer does (or does not) want to "do the same" only if we know *what* is going on, for the viewer, in the depiction. Grimshaw does note that "[i]t should not be supposed that all fantasies have a clear and obvious meaning which can just be read off from some account of the salient features of the narrative."[67] The problem, however, is to specify what the "salient" features of the image are, otherwise we have no grip on "the same." What is salient in the image for this viewer, that which triggers his or her sexual response, may not be what is salient in the image for other viewers, nonusers, antipornography feminists, sexual conservatives, or commission members. What is salient for the viewer might be a detail of the image that is inconsequential in the sight or cognition of, and hence in practice invisible to, these other audiences.

MacKinnon, while voicing in feminist garb an old conservative objection to pornography, is as insensitive to this point as Stoltenberg:

> Sooner or later, in one way or another, the consumer wants to live out the pornography further in three dimensions. Sooner or later, in one way or another, they do. *It* makes them want to; when they believe they can, when they feel they can get away with it, *they* do.[68]

MacKinnon doesn't know anything of the sort. There are many pornographic images that arouse me and bring me sexual pleasure, but I would never actually do what the surface content depicts (nor would I ever dream of *actually* doing them). I doubt that I am alone in this depravity; for one thing, anticipation and fantasy, many learn, are often more exciting than the real thing. But the crucial point is that MacKinnon's claim that men want to and do "live out the pornography" is too crude. What exactly *in* the pornographic image do male viewers want to live out or have a fantasy of doing so? From the fact that the viewer of a pornographic image finds the scenario sexually exciting, we do not know— nor does he, always ("something hooks you about the scene, and you don't necessarily know what")[69]—what it is about or in the depiction that is exciting, what the "trigger" is, or how the viewer remakes the surface content into his or her own fantasy. Hence we cannot say that "this," the surface content *simpliciter*, is what the viewer would like to enact or "live out," were he able to transform fantasy into reality. Of course, that we do not know exactly what large or small detail in the depiction triggers arousal or sexual interest does not mean that the viewer does not want to experience that depiction, in some description or another. It does mean, however, that *any* image, sexual or not, given the right kind of viewer input—be it a photograph of a woman smoking a cigar or passages from the Old Testament—can be an encouragement to copy or do *something*, we know not exactly what. And it also means that even the most surface brutal sadomasochistic pornography does not provide an open window into what its viewers, male or female, would like to occur to or for them in the real world. The failure to afford polysemicity its proper place in the analysis of sexual images is a mistake that goes hand in hand with lacking the ability or willingness to try to understand images, sexual or not sexual, from the perspective of their viewers.[70] Feminists who do that end up with a truncated and exceptionally misleading view of both images and their users, in the same way that the fundamentalist readers of the Bible make that heavy tome into a much less interesting and engaging book.

NOTES

1. Margaret Baldwin, "The Sexuality of Inequality: The Minneapolis Pornography Ordinance," *Law and Inequality: A Journal of Theory and Practice* 2, no. 2 (1984): 631–32.

2. Catharine A. MacKinnon, *Only Words* (Cambridge: Harvard University Press, 1993), p. 27; see also pp. 23–24.

3. Baldwin, "The Sexuality of Inequality," p. 631 n. 11.

4. See Evelyn Fox Keller, *A Feeling for the Organism: The Life and Work of Barbara McClintock* (San Francisco: W. H. Freeman, 1983).

5. Don E. Marietta Jr., *Philosophy of Sexuality* (Armonk, N.Y.: M. E. Sharpe, 1997), p. 117. See also the exaggerations of Alisa L. Carse: "Consider the repeated images in pornography of the

woman spread-eagled, stalked, bound, beaten, mutilated, gagged, or raped" ("Pornography: An Uncivil Liberty?" *Hypatia* 10, no. 1 [1995]: 166); and those of Eva Feder Kittay: "Increasingly, pornographic images depict the torture, mutilation, and even murder of women" ("Pornography and the Erotics of Domination," in *Beyond Domination*, ed. Carol C. Gould [Totowa, N.J.: Rowman and Allanheld, 1984], p. 155).

6. For example, *Only Words*, pp. 15, 17. For the details, see my *Sexual Investigations* (New York: New York University Press, 1996), pp. 238–39.

7. Marty Rimm, "Marketing Pornography on the Information Superhighway," *Georgetown Law Journal* 83 (1995): 1899.

8. Catharine A. MacKinnon, "Vindication and Resistance: A Response to the Carnegie Mellon Study of Pornography in Cyberspace," *Georgetown Law Journal* 83 (1995): 1963.

9. Rimm, "Marketing Pornography," p. 1899.

10. Catharine A. MacKinnon, *Toward a Feminist Theory of the State* (Cambridge: Harvard University Press, 1989), p. 137.

11. MacKinnon, *Only Words*, p. 17; see also *Toward a Feminist Theory*, pp. 136–38, 140, 211; *Feminism Unmodified: Discourses on Life and Law* (Cambridge: Harvard University Press, 1987), pp. 160, 172, 199.

12. Andrea Dworkin, "Why So-Called Radical Men Love and Need Pornography," in *Take Back the Night: Women on Pornography*, ed. Laura Lederer (New York: William Morrow, 1980), p. 148.

13. MacKinnon, *Toward a Feminist Theory*, p. 138. She similarly asserts that women "should study pornography . . . to find out what men really think of them" (Catharine A. MacKinnon, "Preface," in Jeffrey Moussaieff Masson, *A Dark Science: Women, Sexuality, and Psychiatry in the Nineteenth Century* [New York: Farrar, Straus and Giroux, 1986], p. xi).

14. MacKinnon, *Only Words*, p. 21.

15. On MacKinnon's view, says Drucilla Cornell, "[a] man becomes his penis. He cannot help it. The penis asserts itself against him. He is reduced to a prick" ("Pornography's Temptation," in *Feminism and Pornography*, ed. Drucilla Cornell [Oxford: Oxford University Press, 2000], p. 556). Part of Cornell's reply to

MacKinnon is true, but trite (perhaps meant as sarcasm): "I think that men can think and have an erection at the same time" (p. 557).

16. John Stoltenberg, *Refusing To Be a Man: Essays on Sex and Justice* (Portland, Ore.: Breitenbush Books, 1989), pp. 120–21.

17. Ibid., p. 120.

18. Linda Williams, *Hard Core: Power, Pleasure, and the "Frenzy of the Visible"* (Berkeley: University of California Press, 1989), p. x.

19. Both points have been made briefly by Joshua Cohen: "The fact of diversity baffles efforts to identify a single message of pornography"; "Like the fact of diversity, this variation [in "interpretability"] makes it tendentious to suppose that hard-core, sexually explicit expression contains a single message of sexual subordination" ("Freedom, Equality, Pornography," in *Justice and Injustice in Law and Legal Theory*, ed. Austin Sarat and Thomas R. Kearns [Ann Arbor: University of Michigan Press, 1996], pp. 127, 128).

20. Constance Penley, "Crackers and Whackers: The White Trashing of Porn," in *White Trash: Race and Class in America*, ed. Matt Wray and Annalee Newitz (New York: Routledge, 1977), p. 106.

21. To avoid commercial spam, browse newsgroups that contain "nospam" or "moderated" in their names, e.g., alt.binaries. nospam.denim; alt.binaries.nospam.sappho; alt.binaries.erotica. pictures.bondage.moderated.

22. "Compare victims' reports of rape with what pornography says is sex. They look a lot alike. . . . [F]or women it is difficult to distinguish the two ["rape" and "intercourse"] under conditions of male dominance" (MacKinnon, *Toward a Feminist Theory*, pp. 146, 174).

23. Sallie Tisdale had the stubborn courage to invade this male space. See "Talk Dirty to Me," in *The Philosophy of Sex: Contemporary Readings*, 3rd ed., ed. Alan Soble (Lanham, Md.: Rowman and Littlefield, 1997), pp. 271–81.

24. My informal research of pornography available on the Internet was conducted between 1997 and 1999; for study, I viewed thousands upon thousands of images. Most were found free on the newsgroups, which might account for some differences between my observations and those of Marty Rimm's Carnegie Mellon study, which concentrated on pay-site BBS pornography available

in 1994. For example, I found, only for the commercial contributions to the newsgroups, a tremendous disparity between written descriptions of images and the content of those images, while Rimm found, for thirty-five BBSs, that the match between description and image content was 84.5 percent (Rimm, "Marketing Pornography," p. 1890). Maybe my standards of a "match" were more stringent than Rimm's.

25. Ibid., pp. 1906–1907. "Coprophilia" means, literally, "love of feces."

26. Ibid., pp. 1856–57.

27. Robert T. Michael, John H. Gagnon, Edward O. Laumann, and Gina Kolata, *Sex in America* (Boston: Little, Brown and Company, 1994), which is a bowdlerized version of the humongous Edward O. Laumann, John H. Gagnon, Robert T. Michael, and Stuart Michaels, *The Social Organization of Sexuality: Sexual Practices in the United States* (Chicago: University of Chicago Press, 1994).

28. Rimm, "Marketing Pornography," p. 1857 n. 17.

29. See the early version of Kaite's thesis in Sigmund Freud, "Fetishism," in *The Standard Edition of the Complete Psychological Works of Sigmund Freud*, ed. and trans. James Strachey (London: Hogarth Press, 1953–74), vol. 21, pp. 152–57. "The fetish stands for the missing penis of the woman" ("Editor's Note," p. 150).

30. Berkeley Kaite, *Pornography and* Difference (Bloomington: Indiana University Press, 1995), p. ix.

31. Ibid.

32. Ibid., p. 37.

33. Ibid., p. 86.

34. Ibid., p. 50.

35. Ibid., p. 169 n. 1.

36. Linda Williams, "Second Thoughts on *Hard Core*: American Obscenity Law and the Scapegoating of Deviance," in *Dirty Looks: Women, Pornography, Power*, ed. Pamela Church Gibson and Roma Gibson (London: BFI Publishing, 1993), p. 47.

37. Ibid., p. 48.

38. See MacKinnon, *Feminism Unmodified*, pp. 193–95; *Only Words*, pp. 6–7, 40–41, 72–73; *Toward a Feminist Theory*, pp. 205, 247;

and my *Sexual Investigations*, p. 280 n. 7. For MacKinnon, "who listens to a woman with a penis in her mouth?" (*Feminism Unmodified*, p. 193).

39. Williams, "Second Thoughts," p. 58.

40. Mooning is a crime in, for example, Tennessee: "It is a misdemeanor for a person, in a public place . . . to intentionally expose the . . . buttocks to one or more persons" (Tenn. Code Ann. §39-13-511 [1989]); Richard Posner and Katharine Silbaugh, *A Guide to America's Sex Laws* (Chicago: University of Chicago Press, 1996), pp. 94–95.

41. Scott Tucker, "Gender, Fucking, and Utopia," *Social Text* #27 (1990): 28, written in reply to John Stoltenberg's monodimensional reading of pornography. For more on Stoltenberg, see John R. Burger, *One-Handed Histories: The Eroto-Politics of Gay Male Video Pornography* (New York: Haworth Press, 1995), pp. 101–103. "To view pornography as monolithic is to view the variety of sexual experiences as monolithic too" (p. 103).

42. *Final Report of the Attorney General's Commission on Pornography* (Nashville, Tenn.: Rutledge Hill Press, 1986), p. 430.

43. "For me," reported "Becky," a nursery-school teacher of age twenty-five, performing fellatio "is sort of like having him tied up. . . . When a guy's penis is in my mouth, he's absolutely, totally vulnerable. It's the one time I'm totally in control" (quoted by Lillian B. Rubin in her study, *Erotic Wars: What Happened to the Sexual Revolution?* [New York: Farrar, Straus and Giroux, 1990], p. 122).

44. Laumann et al., *Social Organization of Sexuality*, p. 101.

45. Tisdale, "Talk Dirty to Me," p. 280.

46. Dworkin, *Pornography: Men Possessing Women* (New York: Perigee, 1981).

47. See Susan Barrowclough: "It may be that his gaze falls, not on the female genitals (which he may be accustomed to seeing elsewhere) but on the male, and that the chief part of his pleasure, which he may disown subsequently, is homoerotic rather than heterosexual. This ambiguity pornography permits" ("Review of 'Not a Love Story,' " *Screen* 23, no. 5 [1982]: 36). Consider also Sara Diamond's similar claim about women as viewers of pornography:

"While we may be aroused by the sexual activities depicted, most of us cannot avoid identification with the woman in the image, even if we occasionally and sometimes simultaneously identify with the man in the fantasy" ("Pornography: Image and Reality," in *Women Against Censorship*, ed. Varda Burstyn [Vancouver, B.C.: Douglas and McIntyre, 1985], p. 49).

48. On the psychology of being aroused by another's arousal, see Thomas Nagel, "Sexual Perversion," in *The Philosophy of Sex: Contemporary Readings*, 3rd ed., ed. Alan Soble (Lanham, Md.: Rowman and Littlefield, 1997), pp. 9–20.

49. Barrowclough, "Review of 'Not a Love Story,'" pp. 35–36.

50. Rimm, "Marketing Pornography," p. 1886 n. 68.

51. Anne McClintock, "Maid to Order: Commercial S/M and Gender Power," in *Dirty Looks: Women, Pornography, Power*, ed. Pamela Church Gibson and Roma Gibson (London: BFI Publishing, 1993), p. 211. See also Williams, *Hard Core*, p. 196.

52. See my *Pornography: Marxism, Feminism, and the Future of Sexuality* (New Haven, Conn.: Yale University Press, 1986), p. 19 n. 32. The situation hasn't changed since then.

53. McClintock, "Maid to Order," p. 213.

54. Ibid., p. 222.

55. Carole S. Vance, "Negotiating Sex and Gender in the Attorney General's Commission on Pornography," in *Sex Exposed: Sexuality and the Pornography Debate*, ed. Lynne Segal and Mary McIntosh (New Brunswick, N.J.: Rutgers University Press, 1993), p. 43.

56. David M. Halperin, *Saint Foucault: Towards a Gay Hagiography* (Boston: Beacon Press, 1995), p. 90.

57. For example, see the *Final Report*, pp. 430–31, where it provides a review of the magazine *Bizarre Climax No. 9*. According to the review, the magazine depicts in "graphic and nauseating detail the use of urine and feces in sadomasochistic sexual activities" among women (p. 430). The objective language in this review of an exhibit is commendable.

58. Williams, *Hard Core*, p. 205.

59. Laura Kipnis, *Bound and Gagged: Pornography and the Politics of Fantasy in America* (New York: Grove Press, 1996), p. 196.

60. Gayle Rubin, "Misguided, Dangerous and Wrong: An Analysis of Anti-Pornography Politics," in *Bad Girls and Dirty Pictures: The Challenge to Reclaim Feminism*, ed. Alison Assiter and Avedon Carol (London: Pluto Press, 1993), p. 22. See also the widely reprinted essay by Pat Califia, "Feminism and Sadomasochism," in, for example, *Feminism and Sexuality: A Reader*, ed. Stevi Jackson and Sue Scott (New York: Columbia University Press, 1996), pp. 230–37; and Thomas S. Weinberg, ed., *S & M: Studies in Dominance and Submission* (Amherst, N.Y.: Prometheus Books, 1995).

61. McClintock, "Maid to Order," p. 226.

62. Eileen O'Neill, "(Re)presentations of Eros: Exploring Female Sexual Agency," in *Gender/Body/Knowledge: Feminist Reconstructions of Being and Knowing*, ed. Alison M. Jaggar and Susan R. Bordo (New Brunswick, N.J.: Rutgers University Press, 1989), p. 85. Gayle Rubin, McClintock, and O'Neill apparently interpret sadomasochism as largely culturally determined in its meanings and practices. But consider, by contrast, Camille Paglia's take on sadomasochism:

> Sadomasochism is a sacred cult, a pagan religion that reveals the dark secrets of nature. The bondage of sadomasochism expresses our own bondage by the body, our subservience to its brute laws, concealed by our myths of romantic love. . . . It is nature, not society, that is our greatest oppressor.

Sex, Art, and American Culture (New York: Vintage Books, 1992), pp. 44–45.

63. See Susan Farr, "The Art of Discipline," in *Coming to Power*, ed. Samois (Palo Alto, Calif.: Up Press, 1981), p. 184; my *Pornography*, p. 114; and my *Sexual Investigations*, pp. 2–3.

64. See Vance, "Negotiating Sex and Gender in the Attorney General's Commission on Pornography," pp. 44–45.

65. Jean Grimshaw, "Ethics, Fantasy and Self-Transformation," in *The Philosophy of Sex: Contemporary Readings*, 3rd ed., ed. Alan Soble (Lanham, Md.: Rowman and Littlefield, 1997), p. 180.

66. Lynne Segal, "Does Pornography Cause Violence? The Search for Evidence," in *Dirty Looks: Women, Pornography, Power,*

ed. Pamela Church Gibson and Roma Gibson (London: BFI Publishing, 1993), p. 14. See also Elizabeth Cowie: "We cannot assume . . . that the man watching the pornography film showing scenes of violence identifies only, if at all, with the male (or female) figure who conducts the violence. The wish for a passive position in the sexual relationship . . . is extremely common in male sexual fantasies" ("Pornography and Fantasy: Psychoanalytic Perspectives," in *Sex Exposed: Sexuality and the Pornography Debate*, ed. Lynne Segal and Mary McIntosh [New Brunswick, N.J.: Rutgers University Press, 1993], p. 145).

67. Grimshaw, "Ethics, Fantasy and Self-Transformation," p. 180.

68. MacKinnon, *Only Words*, p. 19. See Roger Scruton's similar hysteria: "The harmless wanker with his video-machine can at any moment turn into the desperate rapist with a gun" (*Sexual Desire: A Moral Philosophy of the Erotic* [New York: Free Press, 1986], p. 346).

69. Kipnis, *Bound and Gagged*, p. 197.

70. One more small example of how some feminists misread men through a failure of empathetic identification. (The topic is explored again, in another context, at the end of chapter 3.) Melinda Vadas speaks about "the common man's use of pornographic material as a sex partner," and she asks, "Where pictures can actually be sex partners to men, isn't something ontologically very strange going on?" ("The Pornography/Civil Rights Ordinance v. The BOG: And the Winner Is . . . ?" *Hypatia* 7, no. 3 [1992]: 96.) Yes, something extraordinarily strange would be going on, were men to conceive of pornographic images of women as "sexual partners." This strangeness is good reason to reject the claim, but not for Vadas, who thinks men are weird. As far as I can tell, men do not conceive of or use pornographic images as "sex partners." Is a pillow or my hand a sex partner, if I use them during masturbation? Rae Langton, too, asserts this incredible thesis: "pornography is used as a sexual partner. . . . It is uncontroversial that pornography is used as a sexual partner" ("Sexual Solipsism," *Philosophical Topics* 23, no. 2 [1995]: 152, 180). Uncontroversial? I am not even sure what the claim is supposed to mean, and Langton never provides an account of "sexual partner" that would clarify it. Vadas and

Langton expand the concept of "sex partner" unmercifully, the way that Monica Lewinsky and Bill Clinton unmercifully shrunk the concept of "sex" itself. That men conceive of pornographic images of women as sexual partners is what a woman or feminist might uncharitably *imagine* about men and pornography.

TWO

DEHUMANIZATION, OBJECTIFICATION, ILLUSION

Not to appear a hypocrite I can tell you that a good pair of buttocks is possessed of greater power than all that has ever proceeded from philosophers.

Aretino, *Sei Giornate*[1]

MACKEREL

The power of the buttocks: Sky is wearing tight hot pants on the stage at Onyx, a black strip club in New Orleans East. The hot pants dig deeply into her long crack, emphasizing the roundness and firmness of her ass, and suggesting the genitals and anus that lie below. The men in the audience treasure her ass and the way she shakes it while dancing. The preceding ecdysiasts had been good, but are nothing compared with Sky. By the end of her first number, the men are aroused and excited, but they go nuts when they hear the opening strains of Juvenile's "Back That Azz Up" and realize that Sky would be, in her second number, displaying her fantastic ass accompanied by that provocative tune. The men, spontaneously and in unison, losing themselves in the erotic moment, shower the stage with money as Sky gyrates her ass, sticks it out, bends over, and eventually removes her hot pants to reveal the most enticing backside the men would see for a long time. They stare in awe, objectifying her ass. Sky is fully complicit in this adoration of her backside, proud of her buttocks and gladly showing the men what they want to see. Here the men's look, the objectification of her ass, acknowledges sex as sex, torn from any romantic connections between sex and the "finer" feelings of love, kindness, or consideration. It is this direct sexual look, a look that objectifies and takes no account of "finer" feelings, that feminist and conservative antipornographers find ghastly, the recognition of sex as sex, and as nothing other than sex.[2] As Aretino recognizes, Sky's ass has more power over these men—perhaps only Socrates could resist—than the most exciting passages from Plato, Hume, Kant, Wittgenstein, Putnam, and Kripke. Maybe that's why the feminist antipornographers find displays like Sky's so upsetting. If men are moved foremost by a firm ass, if men, equivalently, are not moveable by the heights of philosophy, little will they be moved by the personalities and intelligences of ordinary women.

But let us not get carried away by the beauty of the buttocks. The fundament also stinks, and for every fantastic ass there are thousands of flabby or skinny and repulsive asses. It is not unfair or far-fetched to insist that the human body is, as far as aesthetic objects go, actually disgusting: Its blemishes, pores, bumps, odors, and fluids are revolting. "[O]ur bodies degenerate, fornicate, secrete, excrete, suppurate, die, and rot."[3] Pornography (and the dancing Sky) obsessively tries to conceal the ugliness of the body by prettifying it, by magnifying its attractions and minimizing its crudeness. Pornography often succeeds at this task. "Sight," as when viewing pornography, "gives us the distance desire must have to operate, back far enough so that smells can be masked and shameful things alluringly covered."[4] True enough, but sight can reveal disgusting things as well. (How can we look at a photograph of the genitals without imagining their odor? Maybe that is the appeal, to *imagine* the odor, modified, made fearless and fragrant, according to the tastes and memory of the viewer.) And even if pornographic beauty is, and is known by the viewers to be, partially concocted with attire and the airbrush, it can anyway send them into paroxysms of sexual joy and awe. Sometimes pornography, instead, wallows in the dirtiness of the body and evokes the sexual excitement associated with that. The anus, mouth, and genitalia can be both beautiful and disgusting, and maybe their appeal is, like sweet-and-sour Chinese, exactly that biting or burning combination.[5]

Further, the human mind is just as disgusting as the human body: Its irrationalities, stupidities, character flaws, and vices are legion and appalling. Everything else, genres other than pornography, seem obsessively concerned to make our minds and characters look better than they are: films of the *It's a Wonderful Life*, *The Sound of Music*, and *Life Is Beautiful* variety upliftingly applaud the nobility, strength, and beauty of the human spirit. Plato wondered, "What if a man had eyes to see the true beauty—the divine beauty, I mean, pure and clear and unalloyed, not infected with the pollutions of the flesh and all the colors and vanities of mortal life?"[6] With or without such eyes, *we* have very little beauty and goodness to see, either of body or mind. "The vast masses seem to be mackerel or herring," lamented D. H. Lawrence.[7] And as Søren Kierkegaard contended (not lamenting, but accepting the hard facts), there is little to admire or respect or love in humans, male or female.[8]

To complain that pornography presents women as "fuck objects"[9] is to presuppose that women, as humans or persons, are something substantially more than fuck objects. Whence this piece of illusory optimism? Pornography is misogynist, but only derivatively, for pornography is, more generally, misanthropic; it recognizes or admits, even in the attempt to deny or conceal it, how disgusting the human is. Pornography is therefore also misandronist, treating its males the same way, as nothing but sexual creatures. Pornography gives to no one, male or female, the respect that no one, male or female, deserves anyway. It demolishes human pretensions. It objectifies that which does not deserve not to be objectified. It thereby repudiates norms that Christian, Western culture holds dear, that people are not to be used or treated as objects or objectified or dehumanized or degraded. Filmmaker and media critic Laura Kipnis understands pornography as rebellion against these norms:

> Its audience is drawn to it because it provides opportunities . . . for the experience of transgression, utopian aspirations, sadness, optimism, loss; and even the most primary longings for love and plenitude. . . . [P]ornography provides a forum to engage with a realm of contents and materials exiled from public view and from the dominant culture, and this may indeed encompass unacceptable, improper, transgressive contents, including, at times, staples of the unconscious like violence, misogyny, or racism. . . . [W]ithin this realm of transgression, there's the freedom . . . to indulge in a range of longings and desires without regard to the appropriateness and propriety of those desires, and without regard to social limits on resources, object choices, perversity, or on the anarchy of the imagination.[10]

Kipnis seems to presuppose that dehumanization, treating people as objects, *is* to lessen them, that doing so is morally wrong, and that pornography allows viewers to transgress these justified or legitimate norms in a peaceful, harmless way. Ian Jarvie apparently has the same thought in mind:

In fantasy we conjure with possibilities without the intrusion of responsibility and consideration. . . . That [men and women] should seek an outlet, dream about and become excited over imaginary scenarios in which responsibility and co[n]sideration can be disregarded, seems harmless enough.[11]

There is a great deal of truth in this view. It is a kind of mainstream liberal line on pornography, the kind of line Catharine MacKinnon vociferously rejects. The line assumes a neat and even plausible distinction between fantasy and reality, between thought and action, and, while admitting that certain sexually dehumanizing actions are morally repugnant and in many cases the fitting province of the criminal law, it insists that mental states per se, the realm of ideation, of conscious and unconscious imaginings, must not only be immune from legal tampering but also have value to the individual despite, and sometimes even because of, their noxious contents.

But, in addition to and going farther than this liberal line, there may be little or no transgression at all in pornographic images or the pornographic imagination, *not really*, or only transgression against social illusions, not against an objective moral truth that society has somehow stumbled upon. If "to degrade is to lower the position, rank, or standing of a person or a group . . . [or] to lower their status,"[12] and if people do not have the ample and lofty metaphysical or moral status we are accustomed to think they have, then they cannot be degraded, not even by pornography. The claim that we should treat people as "persons" and not dehumanize them is to reify, is to anthropomorphize humans and consider them more than they are. Do not treat people as objects, we are told. Why not? Because, goes the answer, people *qua persons* deserve not to be treated as objects. What a nice bit of illusory human chauvinism. People are not as grand as we make them out to be, would like them to be, or hope them to be. Some people desire to be sexually degraded, objectified, and used—so say Eurythmics[13]—but these people as well think too highly of themselves. They sincerely imagine that they do have the dignity that is the prerequisite for them to be degraded in their sexual activities, as does the woman who wrote to Ann Landers, "There are many of us who consider sex an unhygienic and degrading experience that must be endured in order to produce children."[14] Kantian respect for the dignified or dignifiable human lacks the dignified or dignifiable human who could be an appropriate recipient of respect and hence of degradation: Most people in the real world are dirty, fat, ugly, dumb, ignorant, selfish, thoughtless, unreliable, shifty, unrespectable mackerel.[15] Voltaire's character Candide whimsically wonders—he knows the answer—if humans will always be "liars, cheats, traitors, ingrates and thieves, weak, fickle, cowardly, envious, greedy, drunken, miserly, ambitious, bloodthirsty, slanderous, lecherous, fanatical, hypocritical and foolish."[16] But, we are forever told, human dignity is something all people have *qua persons*, something that exists beyond and independent of their variable empirical qualities. "The value of the person as such must be clearly distinguished from the particular values present in a person... [which] are either inborn or acquired," writes Pope John Paul II,[17] postulating a supremely metaphysical and mysterious human dignity. In seeming to violate the prohibition on dehumanization and objectification, pornography proclaims that humans are not so hot after all, that this transcendental value or substance is nonexistent. Pornography, more accurately, rejects (in, say, a transvaluation of value) rather than violates these cherished, self-serving, and self-deceptive moral values. In favoring the enhancement of our perception of the human body, in selecting for display the 5 percent who are beautiful (as de Sade's libertines do at the beginning of the orgy of *The 120 Days of Sodom*), pornography fastens onto something tangible and unmysterious. Of course physical beauty fades, but along with the inevitable procreation that keeps our factories and offices staffed comes the procreation that generates new waves of refreshing beauty.

Feminist Kants

Listen to the feminist philosopher Eva Kittay's confident announcement of the Kantian moral principle she employs to condemn pornography:

> Regardless of how we draw the line between a legitimate and illegitimate sexuality, it appears that there are non-sexual grounds, purely moral considerations which apply to human actions and intentions, that render some sexual acts illegitimate—illegitimate by virtue of the moral impermissibility of harming another person and particularly for the purpose of obtaining pleasure or other benefit from the harm another incurs. Such a moral injunction is but a particular statement of the Kantian imperative not to treat persons as means only. Therefore, I maintain that sexual activity involving the violation of such moral imperatives is *necessarily* illegitimate. . . . [This] illegitimacy . . . derives not from any particular sex/gender system, but from a universal moral imperative.[18]

Kittay offers us a "universal" (in the normative sense, not the descriptive sense) moral principle, according to which some actions are not merely illegitimate, but "necessarily" illegitimate. Whatever the dubious distinction is between the illegitimate and the necessarily illegitimate, Kittay intends to pound us with the monstrousness of actions that are wrong by her Kantian principle. All Kittay does is to take Kant's word for it. There is a cute and not-so-ironic confluence between the radical feminist Kittay and Catholicism: Pope John Paul II, another Kantian philosopher, has asserted, using similar language, that "[s]exual relations outside marriage automatically put one person in the position of an object to be used by another"; "without the institution of *matrimonium* the person is necessarily degraded in the sexual relationship to the status of an object."[19] There is a fundamental agreement here between the feminist Kittay and the Catholic pope, even if each uses the indeterminate concept of treating a "person" as an "end" in his or her own particular ways and to his or her own distinct advantage. I do not deny that harming others is, ceteris paribus, and on a suitably narrow notion of "harm," morally questionable. But to trot out a notion of "necessarily" wrong actions based on a universal moral principle about the immorality of treating people as means or objects is not only logically unnecessary but psychologically and politically suspicious. On a mission to cleanse the world of what she takes to be antiwoman, antifeminist sexual images, Kittay trades in illusions. At least, apparently, she convinced herself.

Professional philosophers are much impressed with their own ethical views. Without a shred of serious investigation, be it anthropological, psychological, historical, or conceptual, the philosopher Judith Hill alleges, in her discussion of pornography, that "[a] person does not have to earn the right to be treated as an end in himself, to be treated with fairness and consideration. . . . These are rights a person has simply in virtue of being a person. . . . Consequently, degradation is always morally wrong."[20] *Simply in virtue of being a person*— as if that claim were transparent in its meaning, obvious in its truth, and didn't beg all sorts of questions. Similarly, John Paul II asserts that the real value of a person, in virtue of which degradation is morally wrong, is "the value of the person as such."[21] This Kantian transcendental value of the person as such is precisely the illusion, whether it exists as a religious or a secular dogma. The noted Kant scholar H. J. Paton, while sympathetically explicating (but not rigorously defending, which seems beyond his, but not only his, abundant powers) Kant's notion of human dignity, inadvertently gives the game away:

> [E]ven when men are far from being saints or heroes, they still have a right, not perhaps to reverence but at least to respect, simply in virtue of their humanity.

How can this be, as Hill also claims, *simply in virtue of their humanity*? Paton continues:

> Merely as human beings they contain the law in themselves at least potentially—that is, they are aware (or at least can be aware) that they ought to obey the law and so must assume themselves free to do so. This is what constitutes the dignity of man, which we have a duty to respect both in ourselves and in others. Every man has a corresponding right to be respected in his dignity as a man.[22]

The parenthetical clause in Paton's hazy even if eloquent explication of Kant demonstrates the thinness of this account of human dignity. It is not that humans *are* actually aware of their duties and hence *do* assume they are free. Instead, the dignity of the human person resides in the fact that humans *could* (might, potentially) acknowledge the moral law and so *could* (might, potentially) sense their duties and assume their own free will to obey or disobey. Exactly what it would take to bridge the gap between the possibility that humans might do or experience any of these things (which is itself doubtful) and their having a right to be treated with respect is unclear. If the point is that we must treat people with respect so that they will develop their ability, and actualize their potential, to perceive their duties and see themselves as free, then to treat people with respect would be, paradoxically, to treat them paternalistically, as if they were infants. But Kantian respect for the other as a person has always seemed to me to exclude paternalism: Treating an adult person as a child is to lessen that person's dignity, is not to recognize it and act accordingly.[23]

Capitalizing on her undefended judgment about degradation that is "always morally wrong," Hill condemns that which she calls "victim pornography," which includes

> the graphic depiction of situations in which women are degraded by sexual activity, . . . situations in which a woman is treated by a man (or by another woman) as a means of obtaining sexual pleasure, while he shows no consideration for her pleasure or desires or well-being.[24]

Think of it: showing no consideration for her sexual pleasure. A major degradation indeed. "Victim Pornography [also] . . . depicts women . . . as eager to be used and abused, totally lacking in human dignity: as more or less worthless for any purpose other than casual sexual intercourse."[25] Yes, that is the premise of misanthropic pornography: no one has or deserves the evasive human dignity that Hill assumes they have or deserve, that humans have value largely only as sexual creatures. Hill provides no argument for, no reasons to take seriously, the idea that women (or men) have any substantial value beyond their value as providers of sexual pleasure, or that being merely or primarily a provider of sexual pleasure is incompatible with human dignity. Anyway, isn't being a provider of sexual pleasure an important and valuable attribute, one to be cherished? Maybe we should construct a theory of human dignity based on our sexual capacities (not "be fruitful and multiply" but "suck, fuck, and be happy"), instead of looking for something "finer" beyond or above the sexual. Hill observes that "Victim Pornography . . . implies that most women are mindless, masochistic nympho-maniacs." She replies to herself, too emphatically, by exclaiming that "[m]ost women are *not* mindless, masochistic nymphomaniacs" (her italics).[26] Note that the implication of Hill's reply is that some women *are* mindless, masochistic nymphomaniacs. Hence, for Hill, the message of victim pornography is false; there are for women higher callings, and some women achieve them. I would have thought, how-ever, that being a mindless, masochistic slut might well be an achievement, something good, at least as good as being, say, a professor of philosophy at a third-rate American university. I don't share Hill's self-serving illusion that having such a high profession is, all things considered, a better state of being and more in keeping with human dignity.[27] At least the slut challenges, and might be the antidote to, the cultural image of women as passive, asexual, pure, whole. This female professor manages only to reinforce the stereotype of academics as stuffy, boring, irrelevant, pretentious, mechan-ical, and utterly lacking creative inspiration.

What bothers Hill about pornography bothers many fem-inists. The sociologist Diana Russell is one of them:

> *Sexual objectification* is another common characteristic of pornography. It refers to *the portrayal of human beings—usu-ally women—as depersonalized sexual things such as "tits, cunt, and ass," not as multi-faceted human beings deserving equal rights with men.*[28]

Who among us, male and female alike, is a "multi-faceted human being," whatever that drippy phrase means? Yeah, our lives are full of different things, the time slots of our lives are filled in with diverse activities. We clock in at the plant, goof off in the men's or ladies' room, clock out of the plant, watch TV at home, go to the bar or the bowling alley or the mall. Or we teach our class, shop at Whole Foods, have a cappuccino at the museum café, and at home slip in a Bach CD. Even if some people are or could be multifaceted, or have value beyond the sexual, must that always be proclaimed and recognized? How dreary, but I suppose so, if dehumanization is always or necessarily wrong. However, we can't always be "good," and no one should expect us to be. A little otherwise harmless dehumanization every once in a while benefits the character; it is a useful, humbling reminder of our true corrupt natures as mackerel or herring.

Rae Langton, who has published a lot of analytic philosophy in defense of Catharine MacKinnon, also trots out the objection:

> Someone might view a person as thing-like: view her not merely as lacking in responsibility, but view her as if there were nothing more to her than appearance, nothing more to her than how she looks, and how she generally manifests herself to the senses. Someone might view a person as being nothing more than a body, nothing more than a conveniently packaged bundle of eyes, lips, face, breasts, buttocks, legs.[29]

So? What is this fantastic "more" that women (and men) are supposed to be or have? There are women (and men) who excel at being nothing more (or nothing less) than a package of sensory experiences, who enjoy being that package, who realize they have absolutely nothing else to offer the world than being that package, and who are grateful that they temporarily have at least this value, instead of nothing. This is not a value at which to sneer, for humans are largely physically ugly. Then there are those women who have absolutely nothing else to offer the world but their nice package, regret that fact, and convince themselves that they must be worth more than that, that they can be professors or lawyers or dentists or attain some other lofty social position. Some of them, failing to obtain anything of worldly value in life, and prompted by MacKinnonites (for example, their opportunistically misleading presentation of legal cases about pornography and of the social science research purportedly documenting its harmful effects),[30] will blame pornography for encouraging men to see them as nothing but sex objects, which social obstacle, on their rationalizing view, keeps them from succeeding. And of course there is the obese or ugly woman who doesn't have the package. Pornographic values condemn her. She thinks to herself some version of the Kittay-Hill-Russell-Langton-Pope John Paul II illusion: "It doesn't matter. What is important is that God loves me. I am lovable in His eyes. These worldly faults are meaningless, in light of my true transcendental worth. I am more than my body, which is actually nothing. And why should I care that I never get laid? I am a human being, a person with a deep real self that contains genuine value. I am multifaceted, a whole human being, even if one facet is cloudy or scratched." Søren Kierkegaard's power of expression (or that of his translators) almost convinces *me*:

[W]hatever your fate in erotic love and friendship, whatever your privation, whatever your loss, whatever the desolation of your life which you confide to the poet, the highest still stands: love your neighbor. . . . [Y]ou can easily find him; him you can never lose.[31]

How romantic, and how beautiful. No wonder this kind of seductive thinking is successful in capturing the hearts and allegiance of the worldly unlovable.

The philosopher Ferrel Christensen replies to those feminists who equate "male attraction to female bodies and sex organs with regarding women as being *nothing but* bodies, devoid of feelings and other attributes," by calling such thinking "sophistry."[32] Christensen might be right that men don't really reduce women to nothing but their parts or appearance. If so, it is one kind of feminist paranoia or a projection, which underestimates the mental agility and stability of men, to think that when men look at women's bodies in pornographic images or in life they are not seeing a person at all.[33] I would have thought, by contrast, that men *wrongly*, in agreement with the illusions promulgated by religious authorities and professional philosophers, attribute personhood and dignity and humanity to women, even as they leer at their bodies.[34] But what if some men, in the style of the pornographic view of things, do regard women, some, many, or all, as monofaceted, as good for nothing but sex? Big deal. How many people, really, are good for *anything*? ("Leonardo da Vinci once pointed out, cynically yet probably correctly, that for most people their only useful contribution to society is to their local cesspit.")[35] In the name of trying to establish their version of social equality between men and women, feminist philosophers foist on us the idea that all women, like all men, like all humans, are multifaceted persons worthy of dignity and respect. Further, they can all be lawyers and doctors and avoid sweeping the floor and cleaning the john, if only sexist (or sexist-capitalist) institutions were dismantled. This is precisely what MacKinnon, with her loose rhetoric, implies about women in our society who perform in pornography:

> You don't have women in your freely-consenting model waking up one morning and saying, "Today is the day on which I make a free choice. Today is the day in which I'm

going to decide whether I want to be a brain surgeon, or whether I want to go and find a man and spread my legs for a camera." That isn't how women get into pornography.[36]

In contrast to these illusions about the worth or respectability or awe-inspiring character of human beings, the misanthropy of pornography grants to humans value only as providers of sexual arousal and sexual pleasure. For Pope John Paul II, too, "pornography . . . [has] the object of inducing the reader or viewer to believe that sexual values are the only real values of the person."[37] But the pontiff thinks that pornography is in this way false and hence harmful. Traders in illusions agree, and would not allow pornography to disseminate its dark and terrible vision. In comparison with the sweetness of the feminist antipornographers, however, pornography looks less like mere cynical crankiness and more like commonsensical realism.

Eros

Another feminist philosopher, Helen Longino, also trades in easy platitudes. "A representation of a sexual encounter which is not characterized by mutual respect, in which at least one of the parties is treated in a manner beneath his or her dignity as a human being, is no longer simple erotica," but is to be condemned as degrading pornography. By contrast,

[a] representation of a sexual encounter between adult persons which is characterized by mutual respect is . . . not morally objectionable. Such a representation would be one in which the desires and experiences of each participant were regarded by the other participants as having a validity and a subjective importance equal to those of the individual's own desire and experiences.[38]

How adorable (even I yearn for it on occasion), but how contrary to the nature of sexuality, as the Czech novelist Milan Kundera describes it:

> "Why don't you ever use your strength on me?" she asked. "Because love means renouncing strength," said Franz softly. Sabina realized two things; first, that Franz's words were noble and just; second, that they disqualified him from her love life.[39]

Longino's line on feminist sexuality is as sappy as the vision of Stoltenberg, who opines that *"respect is absolutely essential. In the sex that you have, treat your partner like a real person who, like you, has real feelings."* As opposed to fake feelings? To pornographic sex, Stoltenberg contrasts a smiley-face view of sex, as that which occurs

> between humans such that mutuality, reciprocity, fairness, deep communion and affection, total body integrity for both partners, and equal capacity for choice-making and decision-making are merged with robust physical pleasure, intense sensation, and brimming-over expressiveness.[40]

Of course pornography exhibits and praises nonprocreative sex, sex for its own sake in all its various forms, not only oral and anal sex, but also bizarre fetishes, sex outside marriage, sex without a lasting bond, sex without emotional entanglements, sex on the spur of the moment with complete strangers. It exhibits and praises casual sex for its own sake. But pornography displays not merely nonprocreative and nonmarital sex, as if it were simply anti-Christian in a narrow sense. It also repudiates sex that is blessed by values of love, commitment, emotional bond, personal intimacy, Longino's "mutual respect." That is, pornography repudiates secular versions of Christianity as well. Longino's illusion is that there could or should be such a thing as mutual respect, or that it is essential to the goodness of human sexuality. To the horror of conservatives and feminists alike, pornography celebrates the cold fuck.

But the cold fuck *is* the fuck. In Longino's brand of morally unobjectionable material, she tells us, each participant shows consideration for the interests and needs of the other participant(s), while in degrading or dehumanizing pornography the participants do not show this consideration, do not express mutual respect. This distinction might seem to embrace a vanilla-sex definition of sex, but it is not even an accurate account of sex, and hence won't do justice even to its mildest flavors. Categorizing sexual material and behaviors in terms of "showing consideration" neglects the *sexual* nature of the material and the *sexual* nature of sex itself. It ignores (what Augustine did not) the spontaneous, uncontrollable arousal, the turbulence, the frenzied passion, the involuntary jerkings, the quest for omnipotence, the primitive infantilism, the acquisitiveness, and all the rest of the *eros* in the sexual. What does yearning desire know of showing consideration, except as a means of fulfilling itself? What does the orgasmic peak know of mutual respect? (Women do drift off, occasionally, from their lovers while enjoying their orgasms.) I hope I'd be the last person to encourage unrelentless selfishness in bed, and I don't deny that it is inconsiderate, although not a mortal sin, to interrupt your mate's orgasm with a tickle or derisive laughter. Nor do I deny that affectionate, giving sex can often be good as sex. But to conceive of good and bad sex and, by extension, good and bad pornography in terms of "showing consideration" is childish, naive, and even, if I dare say so, Christianly effeminate. The bland, jejune sexual ethics of "showing consideration" disregards the essentially amoral, Dionysian dimension of the sexual, and should not be acceptable to any kind of feminism that knows how self-centered and demanding and, hence, un-Christian, women can be in bed.

The philosopher Jean Grimshaw has made a similar but more comprehensive point:

> Eroticism . . . does indeed involve power; the power to give pleasure, to dominate the senses of the other, temporarily to obliterate the rest of the world; the power involved in being the person who is desired, the power to demand one's own pleasure. And along with this power go forms of 'submission' (of surrendering, letting go, receiving), or of self-abnegation, of focusing entirely for a while on the pleasure of the other . . . [and of] some sense of 'loss' of the boundaries of the self.[41]

The tenderness and affection of sexual acts is mixed with aggression and submission, but the mind, and society in the superego, does funny tricks in helping affectionate people, both male and female, miss and deny their aggression, their exertion of power, their mastery and submission. To object to pornography because it does not depict the purity of tender, considerate sex, to object to sex that is not altruistic and mushy, is to cake or smear not just purportedly "disrespectful" sex, but ordinary vanilla sex as well, with gooey illusions.

I assume here something like Sigmund Freud's account of illusions—of sweet dreams. On his view, illusions are

> the fulfilments of the oldest, strongest and most urgent wishes of mankind. . . .What is characteristic of illusions is that they are derived from human wishes. . . . Examples of illusions which have proved true are not easy to find. . . . [They are] insusceptible of proof. . . . [J]ust as they cannot be proved, so they cannot be refuted.[42]

What is the illusion that is pertinent here, which we collectively do not allow to be refuted even as it cannot possibly be defended?—the belief that humans are more than their bodies, more than animals, that, therefore, there is something metaphysically special about humans, their essential dignity, their transcendental value, that makes using them, dehumanizing, objectifying them, morally wrong. Kantian ethics, in particular, whether in a Christian or a secular version, is one big exercise in the erection of illusions. (It is today the professional philosopher's job, assisted in the trenches by the theologian, to erect and promulgate these illusions. A notorious exception is Princeton University's Peter Singer.)[43] The frequent objections to pornography on Kantian grounds rely on bare moral intuitions, moral prejudices, that smack of wish fulfillment and successful cultural indoctrination. One of humanity's oldest wishes or hopes is to be more than the animals we are. It is not just pornography that in its sexual objectification denies this wish; sex itself, too, is essentially objectifying. The ballooning and squirting mechanics of the genitals and their proximity to the organs of urination and defecation are cruel manifestations of our animality. Pornography continually reminds us of human animality and its accompanying sexual objectification, facts that we take to be unpleasant; it exposes that which we try to conceal and is thereby an embarrassment to our pretensions. Pornography harshly unmasks the illusion. "Human sex," says Fred Berger, "just *is* a form of animal coupling, and to make more of it is to invite dishonesty and neurosis."[44] Sexual activity of any sort, including masturbation, with or without pornography or other fetish objects, is an animal function. But "there are certain things we just don't want to know about ourselves. . . . These seem to be precisely what pornography keeps shoving right back at us."[45] Pornography frolics gleefully in our animality, or pushes our faces into it, in all its cruddy, filthy variety. It both venerates and sardonically displays the deep and inescapable immersion of the human in the flesh, or the equivalence of the two, in defiance of the doomed Augustinian wish that the human spirit and will (and God's) grace) could raise us above blindly fornicating animals.[46] Arthur Schopenhauer knew better.[47] As does the sexual conservative philosopher Roger Scruton—although it is odd that he understands sexual perversion in terms of the human becoming animal in sex,[48] yet also thinks that the belief in our being more than our bodies, in our being irreplaceable individuals, is a "transcendental" illusion that we hold, and should continue to hold, because it is socially and psychologically beneficial.[49]

If humans are just and already animals, having nothing special about them metaphysically, then humans, in all their sexual interactions with other humans, are in a sense committing Thomas Aquinas's gravest mortal sin, bestiality.[50] Sexual activity between humans and the "lower" animals has for millennia been unyieldingly condemned. MacKinnon, for example, recently complained that

> Women are disproportionately used in violating ways in pornography. More than ninety-nine percent of all bestiality pictures [on the Amateur Action BBS] present women having sex with animals.[51]

And as her two examples of "the most abusive pornography," she mentions precisely "bestiality" (along with "torture").[52] I find it interesting and amusing that to illustrate her claim that women are "used in violating ways in pornography," MacKinnon picks on bestiality images, of all things, instead of her favorite target, male-dominant, female-submissive pornography (perhaps she means "torture" broadly). Is this selection motivated by her finally realizing that in sadomasochistic pornography there is no "disproportion," both men and women getting their due from both men and women? (Even so, that men and women are equally the abused and the abusers in sadomasochistic pornography should not, for MacKinnon, make it any better than it is, or redeem it; the fact that women are pictured in bestiality images much more frequently than men must be, from her own perspective, an irrelevant red-herring.) MacKinnon doesn't *argue for*, that is, defend with some sort of evidence or reasoning, her claim that bestiality is "violating" and "abusive." I find the claim dubious, that sex between a human and a different sort of animal is per se objectionable. MacKinnon's point here is not that the female model might have been coerced, economically or at knifepoint, into performing a sexual act with a dog or a horse, or that she probably downed a six-pack before doing so. Rather, MacKinnon is disapproving of the nature of the act itself; she implies that something about sexual relations between a woman and a dog makes those sexual activities inherently violating and abusive. MacKinnon—this is why she provides no argument—simply expects her readers to join with her in her disgust and outrage at women having sex with animals and at men downloading and viewing these images for their sexual pleasure. She relies on, manipulates, that popular disgust over and outrage at bestiality in making her case against pornography. (That is one source of my amusement; after all these years of her antipornography crusade, MacKinnon has been pushed into a corner and is now clutching at straws.) Is it a genuine philosophical stance, or merely tricky opportunistic rhetoric, that MacKinnon buys into traditional, conservative sexual values about bestiality in order to drum up support for her condemnation of pornography?

Bestiality, as far as I can tell, need not be abusive, violating, or dehumanizing to the human participant, not inherently. Bestiality is condemned because in these sexual activities, in the minds of its critics, the human really does become nothing but a deranged animal, or descends to that vulgar level. But if humans are already and only animals, no "descent" to that mean level is possible, and this reason for objecting to bestiality disappears, leaving only animal liberation sorts of reasons for not screwing around with dogs or fucking them over. Indeed, it is likely that the animals are the (unwilling? cajoled or bribed by the promise of a good meal?) participants that are disproportionately used in violating and abusive ways in pornography, more so than the human men or women. Even Diana E. H. Russell, whose sociological research is often cited by MacKinnon as demonstrating harms that pornography does to women, and who claims that pornography leads to the rape of women,[53] imagines (without much careful thought, it appears) that there could be a type of pornography or sexual material (which she calls "erotica") that is "respectful of all human beings and animals portrayed."[54] Pray tell, however, how does Russell propose to determine when an animal has consented to sexual activity with a human? That the animal is treated with respect (given abundant strokes?), and that the animal experiences pleasure and even has an orgasm, do not mean that the animal at any time was a willing and genuinely happy participant. After all, some women who are abundantly stroked and who experience pleasure during sexual relations with a human male might still have been, for all that, raped, coerced or pressured into sex they unwillingly came to enjoy.

Linda Williams discusses a taped scene in which pornographic performance artist Annie Sprinkle is teaching her audience how to finger a man's asshole. During her lecture, Sprinkle actually fingers a man's ass, a man whose face is not visible. Williams speaks of this as "Annie's 'objectification' of the man's ass." And it is. A man's ass is a thing that can be studied, manipulated, probed, lectured about, and it would be fatuous extravagance for Sprinkle to "show consideration" for or to her exhibit, to utter some uplifting pleasantries, while employing his ass in the demonstration. Williams goes on to make a point about polysemicity. Is Sprinkle teaching women how to do the deed to their men, or teaching a man how to do it to another man or himself, or showing what gives *her* pleasure, to penetrate a man digitally? "Any way you look at it, Annie has played with the conventions of who gives pleasure to whom."[55] The scene also illustrates the objectification of body parts that essentially occurs in sexual activity: If you want to give someone anal pleasure—another person or yourself—you must learn technique, you must learn what the anus is like, you must play and experiment with it. The anus must be seen and treated as a thing separate from the personality or purported dignity of its owner. No doubt this objectification, the reduction in our perspective of the human to its genuine animality, is, given our sincerely and powerfully held illusions, psychologically risky. But life is risky, merely existing is risky, and it is farcical to seek comfort in adopting the undaring cowardice of a J. Alfred Prufrock (the poetical character of T. S. Eliot). The same point—in sexual activity the parts are objectified in the service of effective technique and the sexual pleasure it produces—applies, perhaps more dramatically, to the genital kiss.[56] Only a stupid, self-deceptive, self-centered girl would think to herself, "He loves me; ergo it doesn't matter how I do it (or even if I do it)."[57] Love, concern, or well-meaning attitudes on the part of the fellator or cunnilinguist, even if they might help (instead of, which is just as likely, getting in the way),[58] are no substitute for technique, for sexual knowledge of the way things work. Beyond the Point of First Intercourse, and perhaps even then, it is objectifying technique that makes the act pleasurable instead of a frustrating, fumbling nuisance. This is why marriage and relationship counselors emphasize the importance of communication about sexuality and encourage partners to try saying "A little bit over, please" or "Do it *this* way, honey." Although—the responsibility to know and employ the knowledge of another person's sexual likes and dislikes can be counterproductive: There are "times when it's a relief not to have to listen to somebody's directives about what she wants, and to be worrying all the time" about doing it exactly right and showing proper consideration.[59] (Note how this suggests a motive, also, for the use of pornography for sexual pleasure and trips to one's local prostitute.) The writer bell hooks was nearly right when she said—if she said—that "[w]e can't just ask men to give up sexist objectification if we want a hard dick and a tight butt—and we do."[60] What hooks overlooks is that if women's objectification of males as sexual creatures, as hard dicks and tight butts, is essential to sex, there's no sense calling it "sexist."[61]

NAMES

The philosopher and classicist Martha Nussbaum concedes that sexual congress per se, by its nature, objectifies the participants. One of her proposals for how this objectification can be attenuated is for lovers to humanize their genitals by giving them pet names:

> Giving a proper name to the genital organs of each is a way of signifying the special and individual way in which they desire one another. . . . It is a reminder that the genital organs of people are not really fungible, but have their own individual character, and are in effect parts of the person, if one will really look at them closely without shame. . . . We have to learn to call our genital organs by proper names— that would be at least the beginning of a properly complete human regard for one another.[62]

How prosaic, and how inundated with illusion: let us pretend that our dicks and cunts are grandly human by naming them. The genital organs are described by Nussbaum as if they were in reality what human persons are supposed to be, on a Kantian view: as irreplaceable, as not fungible, as having "individual character." Contra hooks, dicks aren't comparable, worse ones (soft, tiny, wimpy, in hiding) not replaceable in our lust by better ones (hard, big, swollen, pulsating). There is no possibility of "trading up" to a wetter, prettier, more fragrant, cleaner, more accommodating pussy. Each dick and each cunt has its own individual character, if we examine them microscopically. This is true, of course, but trivially. "[A]ny gynecologist, urologist, or pediatrician can tell you that . . . [g]enitals vary a great deal."[63] But we do not need to rely pompously on the scientific testimony of medical personnel for the revelation of this fact; any promiscuous person knows this, as does any serious peruser of pornography. Nussbaum's argument seems to be that the objectification of the human that essentially occurs in sexual congress, the objectification that denies our nonfungibility and individual character, is attenuated by transforming dicks and cunts into persons—dignified persons with proper names— in their own right. This reification of the genitals is more puerile than imagining that humans themselves are Kantian persons. Even if genital organs do have individual character—the wart midway up the shaft of the penis, the distorted asymmetry of the labia—is this uniqueness that which makes them special things in our lives and loves? In the ubiquitously unique and personalized crotch, like a personalized license plate that provides the illusion that its owner is special, we have finally uncovered the elusive ingredient that grounds Kantian respect.[64]

Something more insidious is going on here. Note Nussbaum's claim that "giving a proper name to the genital organs of each is a way of signifying the special and individual way in which they desire one another." She is talking about lovers who know each other, are not strangers who meet in the night or in a bar or museum, about which we can hardly say that they desire each other in a special and individual way. In casual sex, fungibility and replaceability reign. Casual sex is, perhaps, even the paradigm case of sexual congress: more sex, and more sex faithful to the *eros* of sex, probably occurs between strangers or slight acquaintances than between married people, who have often grown bored with their sexual routine and are now immune to the uniqueness of each other's genitals. At least, sex with a stranger or new partner is often more passionate, exciting, and exhilarating than sex with a familiar partner.[65] Nussbaum is not claiming, to her credit, that strangers who meet in the night should stop for a minute in their mutual lust to name their genitals; for her, the naming of the genitals, and the specialness that that event signifies, comes from the already-established specialness of the relationship between the lovers, and helps *them* mollify sexual objectification. When there is no special relationship, the attenuation of the objectification of sexual congress provided by naming the genitals is not available, so casual sex between strangers for Nussbaum remains, in this respect, unredeemed objectification. My guess is that once the *eros* is gone from the sexual relations of the married couple, *that* accounts for the attenuation of sexual objectification in their relationship, not that they have achieved it by naming their genitals.

But does naming the genitals really attenuate or overcome objectification? Michael Kimmel, one of the self-appointed spokespersons of the men's liberation (nonsexist, profeminist) movement, claims that naming the genitals amounts to sexual self-objectification:

> In locker rooms and playgrounds, men learn to detach their
> emotions from sexual expression. Detachment requires
> sexual self-objectification. . . . The penis is transformed
> from an organ of sexual pleasure into a "tool," an instru-
> ment by which the job is carried out, a thing, separate from
> the self. Men have developed a rather inventive assortment
> of nicknames for their penises, including the appropriation
> of real first names, like "John Thomas" and "Peter." (Can
> we imagine a woman calling her vagina "Shirley" or her
> clitoris "Sally Ann"?)[66]

The sexually naive feminist Kimmel, consumed by a political
correctness that sees only goodness in women, cannot
imagine that women give names to their genitals, that they,
too, engage in sexual self-objectification, that they "appropriate" names for their cunts or clits or tits. Of course some
women do name their sexual parts, so it is easy to "imagine"
them doing so. Maybe Kimmel would reply that women par-
take of genital naming without, in contrast to men, its objectifying quality; or they do so under patriarchal compulsion
or as an act of collusion with their oppressive sexual colo-
nizers. That sounds like special pleading. It does seem to me,
however, that Kimmel is on to something, that naming the
genitals, instead of humanizing them, does objectify: In the
process of attempting to raise the status of a mere material,
fleshy thing, naming the genitals acknowledges that what is
an object is an object. Adam's giving names to the lower creatures reinforced—it did not undermine or attenuate—his
objectification of and dominion over them. People who think
that naming their genitals genuinely humanizes them are
committing self-deception. Relying on the resplendence of a
name like "Balzac" or the comforting everydayness or
domesticity of a name like "Jennifer," they try to turn something ugly and beastly into something pretty and tamed.

Note that Kimmel mentions the locker room name "John

Thomas," which is the name given to his penis by Oliver Mellors in D. H. Lawrence's *Lady Chatterley's Lover*. Mellors also gives a name to Connie's cunt:

> "Do you know what I thought?" she said suddenly. "It suddenly came to me. You are the 'Knight of the Burning Pestle'!"
>
> "Ay! And you? Are you the Lady of the Red-Hot mortar?"
>
> "Yes!" she said. "yes! You're Sir Pestle and I'm Lady Mortar."
>
> "All right, then I'm knighted. John Thomas is Sir John, to your Lady Jane." . . .
>
> "That's you in all your glory!" he said. "Lady Jane, at her wedding with John Thomas." . . .
>
> "This is John Thomas marryin' Lady Jane."[67]

Mellors is almost completely in charge, appropriating the right to name both his genitals and hers. Connie is allowed no room of her own in which to exert the power of the word. It is, then, ironic that Nussbaum appeals to this literary example to suggest that naming the genitals humanizes them and attenuates the sexual objectification of sexual congress. That Lawrence's novel does not present a model of how to attenuate sexual objectification in heterosexual relationships is confirmed by another passage in *Lady Chatterley's Lover*:

> "How strange!" she said slowly. "How strange he stands there! So big! and so dark and cock-sure! Is he like that?" . . .
>
> "So proud!" she murmured, uneasy. "And so lordly! Now I know why men are so overbearing! But he's lovely, *really*. Like another being!" . . .
>
> "And now he's tiny, and soft like a little bud of life!" she said, taking the soft small penis in her hand. "Isn't he somehow lovely! so on his own, so strange! And *so* inno-

cent? And he comes so far into me! You must *never* insult him, you know. He's mine too. He's not only yours. He's mine! And so lovely and innocent! . . . And how lovely your hair is here! quite quite different."

"That's John Thomas' hair, not mine!" he said.

"John Thomas! John Thomas!" and she quickly kissed the soft penis, that was beginning to stir again.

"Ay!" said the man, stretching his body almost painfully. "He's got his root in my soul, has that gentleman! An' sometimes I don' know what ter do wi' him. Ay, he's got a will of his own, an' its hard to suit him." . . .

[T]he penis in slow soft undulations filled and surged and rose up, and grew hard, standing there hard and over-weening, in its curious towering fashion. The woman too trembled a little as she watched.

"There! Take him then! He's thine," said the man.

And she quivered, and her own mind melted out.[68]

Despite the fact that Constance Chatterley and Oliver Mellors are hardly strangers to each other, the naming of the penis here makes the organ an impersonal tertium quid, not human, a pagan god to be worshiped. The Lawrentian penis has a detached life and will of its own.[69] Note that in *Lady Chatterley's Lover*, Connie and Oliver never call *each other* by their given proper names. As Connie explains to Hilda, her sister, "I've never called him by any name: nor he me: which is curious, when you come to think of it. Unless we say Lady Jane and John Thomas."[70] ("You Never Even Called Me By My Name," wails David Allen Coe.) Cock and cunt and their congress per se are so important in this relationship that their delicious existence trumps personal identity, or becomes it.[71] "So big!" indeed. Oliver signs his letter to Connie, which closes *Lady Chatterley's Lover*, not with "Ollie" or "your big fucker," but with "John Thomas says good-night to lady Jane, a little droopingly, but with a hopeful heart." In his best prescient MacKinnon routine, Lawrence proclaims that Man is Penis; Woman, Cunt. All told, it seems foolish for Nussbaum to attempt to solve the riddle of sexual objectification by citing Lawrence's novel: The relationship between Constance and Oliver is a sexual one, pure and simple. If there is any truth in *"Rx. Penis normalis dosim repetatur"*—all she needs is a good fuck (literally: "Prescription. A normal penis, dose to be repeated.")—it surely applies to Constance Chatterley (more than it does to Mellors).[72] Their relationship is wondrously shallow, although not to be condemned on that score. Two horny, lonely people meet and screw their brains out, to their mutual satisfaction and, as in *Romeo and Juliet*, to the horror of everyone else. Like a Hollywood romance, however, *Lady Chatterley's Lover* ends too soon, ends before the real story begins, before Connie and Oliver settle down in domestic lethargy.

NOTES

1. Quoted by Achillo Olivieri, "Eroticism and Social Groups in Sixteenth-Century Venice: The Courtesan," in *Western Sexuality: Practice and Precept in Past and Present Times*, ed. Philippe Ariès and André Béjin (Oxford: Blackwell, 1985), p. 96.

2. Note that the polysemicity of Sky's performance allows her to engage in mocking the men even as she is objectified by them. Performances in bars "provide women with the opportunity to invert, caricature, tease, manipulate, and exploit those who use their bodies. . . . The fact that most bar patrons are unaware of the insult [e.g., kiss my ass] only adds to its power" (Leonore Manderson, "The Pursuit of Pleasure and the Sale of Sex," in *Sexual Nature Sexual Culture*, ed. Paul Abramson and Steven Pinkerton [Chicago: University of Chicago Press, 1995], p. 314).

3. William Ian Miller, *The Anatomy of Disgust* (Cambridge: Harvard University Press, 1997), p. 49.

4. Ibid., p. 79.

5. See my *Sexual Investigations* (New York: New York University Press, 1996), pp. 198–204.

6. Plato, *Symposium* 211e; in *Eros, Agape, and Philia: Readings in the Philosophy of Love*, ed. Alan Soble (St. Paul, Minn.: Paragon House, 1989), p. 56.

7. D. H. Lawrence, *Lady Chatterley's Lover* (New York: New American Library, 1962), p. 29.

8. In his explication of *agape*, Søren Kierkegaard claims that the Christian task is to love human beings, who are in a worldly sense unlovable. (Is this universal worldly unlovableness a version of Augustine's original sin?) See Søren Kierkegaard, *Works of Love* (New York: Harper and Row, 1962), pp. 117, 158, 342–43, 377 n. 78, and my discussion in *The Structure of Love* (New Haven, Conn.: Yale University Press, 1990), pp. 133–34. Immanuel Kant might have had the same idea: "To do good to other human beings insofar as we can is a duty. . . . [E]ven if one had to remark sadly that our species, on closer acquaintance, is not particularly lovable, that would not detract from the force of this duty" (*The Metaphysics of Morals*, trans. Mary Gregor [Cambridge: Cambridge University Press, 1996], p. 161).

9. Margaret Baldwin, "The Sexuality of Inequality: The Minneapolis Pornography Ordinance," *Law and Inequality: A Journal of Theory and Practice* 2, no. 2 (1984): 632 n. 12.

10. Laura Kipnis, *Bound and Gagged: Pornography and the Politics of Fantasy in America* (New York: Grove Press, 1996), pp. xii–xiii, 202–203.

11. Ian C. Jarvie, *Thinking about Society: Theory and Practice* (Dordrecht: D. Reidel, 1986), p. 445.

12. Ian C. Jarvie, "Pornography and/as Degradation," *International Journal of Law and Psychiatry* 14 (1991): 13.

13. Listen to the 1982 Eurythmics song "Sweet Dreams (Are Made of This)."

14. "No-Sex Marriage," *Dallas Morning News*, March 11, 1998, p. 2C.

15. A joke I remember hearing on a sitcom rerun:

Woman: You mean that 95 percent of us are "undatable"?
Man: Right.
Woman: Then how do we ever get together?
Man: Alcohol.

We could add to this truth, others: a loneliness that no longer discriminates; a horniness that no longer discriminates; peer group pressure and social and familial expectations to form pairs; fear of death; the desire for children, even ugly ones; two together can live less expensively than two separately; and, perhaps most important, a self-willed blindness to the overpowering defects of the other person, which supplements a self-willed overestimation of the other's few admirable traits, thereby achieving by a dance of the mind the stupor produced by alcohol.

16. Voltaire, *Candide*, trans. Lowell Bair (New York: Bantam Books, 1959), p. 81.

17. Karol Wojtyła [Pope John Paul II], *Love and Responsibility*, trans. H. T. Willetts (New York: Farrar, Straus, Giroux, 1981), p. 122.

18. Eva Feder Kittay, "Pornography and the Erotics of Domination," in *Beyond Domination*, ed. Carol C. Gould (Totowa, N.J.: Rowman and Allanheld, 1984), pp. 150–51. To the last claim in the passage, Kittay attaches an endnote, which begins: "It may be more difficult to justify such a claim on utilitarian grounds or even on the basis of rights" (Ibid., p. 173 n. 7), which implies that Kittay is not a genuine but an opportunistic Kantian: Embracing Kant is the only way, she thinks, she is able to condemn what she has an inclination to condemn. This maneuver is both intellectually and psychologically suspicious, and even Kant would protest.

19. Wojtyła, *Love and Responsibility*, pp. 221, 222.

20. Judith M. Hill, "Pornography and Degradation," in *Pornography: Private Right or Public Menace?*, rev. ed., ed. Robert M. Baird and Stuart E. Rosenbaum (Amherst, N.Y.: Prometheus Books, 1998), p. 103.

21. Wojtyła, *Love and Responsibility*, p. 122; see also p. 298 n. 29.

22. H. J. Paton, "Kant on Friendship," in *Friendship: A Philo-*

sophical Reader, ed. Neera Kapur Badhwar (Ithaca, N.Y.: Cornell University Press, 1993), p. 138.

23. I have no qualms about saying that treating someone as a person or as an end means that we allow him or her to make decisions freely, without coercion, and in the possession of relevant information, without deception or ignorance. But then we do not need the concept of treating someone as a person at all; it is superfluous. And the presence of free and informed consent is not what feminists and conservatives have in mind when they criticize pornography as degrading to the person. For some discussion of in what circumstances treating someone as a person amounts to respecting their autonomous choices, see Nora O'Neill, "Between Consenting Adults," in her *Constructions of Reason: Explorations of Kant's Practical Philosophy* (Cambridge: Cambridge University Press, 1989), pp. 105–25. See also my "Sexual Use and What to Do about It" [online], www.uno.edu/~asoble/pages/essays.htm.

24. Hill, "Pornography and Degradation," pp. 105-106.

25. Ibid., p. 107.

26. Ibid., p. 108.

27. I would thus go farther than Martha Nussbaum's circumspect comparison:

> Both performances involve skill. It might plausibly be argued that the professor's involves a more developed skill, or at least more expensive training—but we should be cautious here. Our culture is all too ready to think that sex involves no skill and is simply "natural," a view that is surely false.

Martha C. Nussbaum, " 'Whether From Reason or Prejudice'. Taking Money for Bodily Services," in her collection *Sex and Social Justice* (New York: Oxford University Press, 1999), p. 284.

28. Diana E. H. Russell, "Introduction," in *Making Violence Sexy: Feminist Views on Pornography*, ed. Diana E. H. Russell (New York: Teachers College Press, 1993), p. 6.

29. Rae Langton, "Sexual Solipsism," *Philosophical Topics* 23, no. 2 (1995): 165. See also John Stoltenberg, *Refusing to Be a Man:*

Essays on Sex and Justice (Portland, Ore.: Breitenbush Books, 1989), p. 48.

30. Here is one portion of a legal decision, written by Judge Frank Easterbrook, frequently cited by MacKinnonites:

> Pornography is an aspect of dominance. . . . There is much to this perspective. . . . People often act in accordance with the images and patterns they find around them. . . . Depictions of subordination tend to perpetuate subordination. The subordinate status of women in turn leads to affront and lower pay at work, insult and injury at home, battery and rape on the streets.

"American Booksellers Ass'n Inc. v. Hudnut, 771 F.2d 323 (1985)," in *In Harm's Way: The Pornography Civil Rights Hearings,* ed. Catharine A. MacKinnon and Andrea Dworkin (Cambridge: Harvard University Press, 1997), p. 472. Also in Lori Gruen and George F. Panichas, eds., *Sex, Morality, and the Law* (New York: Routledge, 1997), pp. 168–69. What is not frequently cited by MacKinnonites is Easterbrook's second footnote, which greatly qualifies his statement above.

31. Kierkegaard, *Works of Love,* p. 76.

32. Ferrel M. Christensen, "Cultural and Ideological Bias in Pornography Research," *Philosophy of the Social Sciences* 20, no. 3 (1990): 360.

33. One example of this fanatical, paranoid feminism will suffice:

> What the men are doing in the world is continuing to *see*— to see women as objects of their pleasure and their feeling of life. It is quite enough 'behaviour' in my opinion. What the man is doing is watching pornography, seeing, fantasizing, and he is doing this already in the world. . . . The fundamental problem at the root of men's behaviour in the world, including sexual assault, rape, wife battering, sexual harassment, keeping women in the home and in unequal opportunities and conditions, treating them as objects for conquest and protection—the root problem behind the reality of men's relations with women, is the way men see women, is Seeing.

Susanne Kappeler, *The Pornography of Representation* (Minneapolis: University of Minnesota Press, 1986), pp. 60–61. She also thinks that "[w]ith lovers like men, who needs torturers?" (p. 214). For more on Kappeler, see my review of her book in *Philosophy of the Social Sciences* 19, no. 1 (1989): 128-31.

34. See my *Sexual Investigations*, pp. 97–98.

35. Ralph A. Lewin, *Merde: Excursions in Scientific, Cultural, and Sociohistorical Coprology* (New York: Random House, 1999), p. 129. As Lewin mentioned, this is not merely a joke: "The experience of waste in sixteenth-century France was an authentic feature of its antique revival. What specifically was revived was not the Greek and Roman cult of excrement, but the intensive use of fecal matters—and above all human feces—in agricultural methods practiced under the first Emperors" (Dominique Laporte, *History of Shit* [Cambridge: MIT Press, 2000], p. 32).

36. Catharine A. MacKinnon, "Testimony before the Los Angeles Hearing (1985)," in *In Harm's Way: The Pornography Civil Rights Hearings*, ed. Catharine A. MacKinnon and Andrea Dworkin (Cambridge: Harvard University Press, 1997), pp. 392–93.

37. Wojtyła, *Love and Responsibility*, p. 192.

38. Helen E. Longino, "Pornography, Oppression, and Freedom: A Closer Look," in *The Problem of Pornography*, ed. Susan Dwyer (Belmont, Calif.: Wadsworth, 1995), p. 36. See also James V. P. Check and Ted H. Guloien, "Reported Proclivity for Coercive Sex Following Repeated Exposure to Sexually Violent Pornography, Nonviolent Dehumanizing Pornography, and Erotica," in *Pornography: Research Advances and Policy Considerations*, ed. Dolf Zillmann and Jennings Bryant (Hillsdale, N.J.: Lawrence Erlbaum, 1989), pp. 159–84: "dehumanizing or degrading pornography" (p. 162) contains depictions of "sexual interactions in which the woman [is] portrayed as hysterically responsive to male sexual demands, [is] verbally abused, dominated, and degraded, and in general treated as a plaything with no human qualities other than her physical attributes" (p. 163); "erotica," by contrast, "consist[s] of scenes of mutually consenting, affectionately oriented sexual interactions" (pp. 163–64).

39. Milan Kundera, *The Unbearable Lightness of Being* (New York: Harper and Row, 1984), p. 112.

40. Stoltenberg, *Refusing To Be a Man*, pp. 37, 112. According to Scott Tucker ("Gender, Fucking, and Utopia," *Social Text* #27 [1990]: 3–34), Stoltenberg expresses "the utopian purity of spirit." He is "intent to take the raw and messy stuff of sex and gender and to draw out the otherworldly quintessence, the pure gold of what could be if only we, too, were pure enough to extract it from a fallen world" (p. 25). Tucker is right to sense Augustine (on the sexuality of prelapsarian Adam and Eve) in Stoltenberg: "Stoltenberg prefers an eroticism so diffuse that it sounds less vigorous than a Swedish massage; in his utopia pain and pleasure are always clearly distinct" (p. 30).

41. Jean Grimshaw, "Ethics, Fantasy and Self-Transformation," in *The Philosophy of Sex: Contemporary Readings*, 3rd. ed., ed. Alan Soble (Lanham, Md.: Rowman and Littlefield, 1997), p. 182. On "sexually constitutive masochism," see Leo Bersani, "Is the Rectum a Grave?" *October* 43 (winter 1987): 217; and his *The Freudian Body: Psychoanalysis and Art* (New York: Columbia University Press, 1986), pp. 39, 89, and 41: "[S]exuality would not be originally an exchange of intensities between individuals, but rather a condition in which others merely set off the self-shattering mechanisms of masochistic *jouissance*."

42. Sigmund Freud, *The Future of an Illusion*, in *The Standard Edition of the Complete Psychological Works of Sigmund Freud*, ed. and trans. James Strachey (London: Hogarth Press, 1953–74), vol. 21, pp. 30–31.

43. See, for example, Michael Specter, "The Dangerous Philosopher," *New Yorker* (September 6, 1999): 46–55.

44. Fred R. Berger, "Pornography, Sex, and Censorship," in *The Philosophy of Sex: Contemporary Readings*, 1st ed., ed. Alan Soble (Totowa, N.J.: Rowman and Littlefield, 1980), p. 329.

45. Kipnis, *Bound and Gagged*, p. 171.

46. "[B]y the final meeting of the Commission, pornography had become a matter of moral concern to me. . . . I remembered something about the higher purposes of life and of humanity's

aspirations" (Park Elliott Dietz, "Statement of Park Elliott Dietz," *Final Report of the Attorney General's Commission on Pornography* [Nashville, Tenn.: Rutledge Hill Press, 1986], p. 488). Dietz was one of the members of the commission.

47. Arthur Schopenhauer, *The World as Will and Representation*, trans. E. F. J. Payne (Indian Hills, Colo.: Falcon's Wing Press, 1958), vol. 2, pp. 538–40.

48. Roger Scruton, *Sexual Desire: A Moral Philosophy of the Erotic* (New York: Free Press, 1986), p. 27.

49. See my *The Structure of Love*, pp. 296–97, 321 n. 2, 330 n. 40, 353 n. 17.

50. On Aquinas and bestiality, see my *Sexual Investigations*, pp. 10–11, and my *The Philosophy of Sex and Love: An Introduction* (St. Paul, Minn.: Paragon House, 1988), pp. 28–29. The animals we are, are the Bonobos, or they are us. For a brief introduction, see Meredith F. Small, "Prime Mates: The Useful Promiscuity of Bonobo Apes," *Nerve* [www.nerve.com/small/bonobo/bonobo. html]. See also, with photographs of nasty acts, Frans B. M. de Waal, "Sex as an Alternative to Aggression in the Bonobo," in *Sexual Nature Sexual Culture*, ed. Paul Abramson and Steven Pinkerton (Chicago: University of Chicago Press, 1995), pp. 37–56.

51. Catharine A. MacKinnon, "Vindication and Resistance: A Response to the Carnegie Mellon Study of Pornography in Cyberspace," *Georgetown Law Journal* 83 (1995): 1963. MacKinnon didn't examine this BBS pornography herself; she took her data from Marty Rimm, "Marketing Pornography on the Information Superhighway," *Georgetown Law Journal* 83 (1995): 1849–1934.

52. MacKinnon, "Vindication and Resistance," p. 1965.

53. Diana E. H. Russell, "Pornography and Rape: A Causal Model," *Political Psychology* 9, no. 1 (1988): 41–73.

54. Russell, "Introduction," p. 3 (italics deleted).

55. Linda Williams, "A Provoking Agent: The Pornography and Performance Art of Annie Sprinkle," in *Dirty Looks: Women, Pornography, Power*, ed. Pamela Church Gibson and Roma Gibson (London: BFI Publishing, 1993), pp. 184–85.

56. On the objectifying nature of oral sex, see my *Sexual Inves-*

tigations, pp. 216–17, 224–25. My idea here, that human sexuality is already by its essence objectifying, is denied, for example, by the feminist philosopher Melinda Vadas:

> Pornography . . . creates and maintains a practice of the sexual in which male arousal is cued or keyed by the objective presentation of femaleness. (You know, all those cunt shots.) . . . Thus pornography creates and maintains the sort of male desire that is satisfied by the consumption of objective femaleness, and thus it creates and maintains the sort of male desire that objectifies flesh-and-blood women. . . . In keying male arousal to the objective presentation of female biological sexedness (i.e., pussy), pornography creates and maintains a practice of the sexual within which rape is not a *conceptually* deviant practice, even if it is considered to be a morally deviant practice.

"The Pornography/Civil Rights Ordinance v. The BOG: And the Winner Is. . . ?" *Hypatia* 7, no. 3 (1992): 96–97.

Vadas provides no argument for her astounding thesis, that pornography conditions (cues, keys) men's sexual desire to female-part-as-object, that men's objectifying interest in the female genitals is "created" by sexual materials. Sex itself, by its nature, is already plenty full of objectification, and surely men's wanting to look at and inspect female genitalia was not created by pornography; it has existed and will continue to exist quite well without any pornography to fuel it. Does Vadas really think—which is implied by her claim—that were pornography to eschew the cunt or pussy shot altogether and to depict, instead, only whole-bodied women, that would reduce men's sexual objectification of women?

Note, also, Vadas's expression "creates and maintains." The claim that society, or this or that part of it, creates and maintains something uncongenial to feminists, something patriarchal or sexist, is, in their writings, a common stratagem. Here's another example:

> Prostitution . . . is a practice that is constructed by and reinforces male supremacy, which both creates and legitimizes

the "needs" that prostitution appears to satisfy. . . . [C]api-
talist and patriarchal conditions . . . create both the male
needs themselves and the ways in which women fill them.

Christine Overall, "What's Wrong with Prostitution? Evaluating
Sex Work," *Signs* 17, no. 4 (1992), p. 724.

I think that illusions underlie such feminist thinking. They
accept uncritically the non sequiturs that if an aspect of human
existence is biological, then it is unchangeable, but if it is socially
generated, it can be done away with. Then, in a flight of optimism,
they put their most hated sexist institutions and practices into the
social category, thereby ensuring that, with enough political
activism and social engineering, these items will wither away. I do
not mean, of course, that these nefarious items should remain on
the scene; I object only to the style of reasoning, which seems to me
self-deluded.

57. According to Kierkegaard, the wife shows her love for her
husband just by doing something for him, no matter how well (or
poorly) she does it, because it is the intention behind her act that
counts—to please him—and the husband should be wholly happy
at the attempt and ignore its efficacy:

[I]f she were to adorn herself merely to please him. . . . —if
he with a single nerve of his eye were to see amiss and
admire, instead of comprehending love's correct expression, that it was to please him, already he is on a false track,
he is on the point of becoming a connoisseur.

"Various Observations about Marriage, in reply to objections, by a
married man," in *Stages on Life's Way* (Princeton, N.J.: Princeton
University Press, 1945), p. 157.

58. This is one of the themes of Russell Vannoy's *Sex Without Love:
A Philosophical Exploration* (Amherst, N.Y.: Prometheus Books, 1980).

59. Martin, a lawyer of age thirty-eight years, quoted by Lillian B. Rubin in her study, *Erotic Wars: What Happened to the Sexual
Revolution?* (New York: Farrar, Straus and Giroux, 1990), p. 122.

60. Quoted by Tad Friend, "Yes," *Esquire* (February 1994): 56.

61. See Avedon Carol and Nettie Pollard, "Changing Percep-

tions in the Feminist Debate," in *Bad Girls and Dirty Pictures: The Challenge to Reclaim Feminist*, ed. Alison Assiter and Avedon Carol (London: Pluto Press, 1993), p. 47.

62. Martha C. Nussbaum, "Objectification," in *The Philosophy of Sex: Contemporary Readings*, 3rd ed., ed. Alan Soble (Lanham, Md.: Rowman and Littlefield, 1997), pp. 303–304. "Why do men name their penises? Because they want to be on a first-name basis with the person who makes all their decisions," is a cute MacKinnonish joke (Mary-Lou Zeitoun, "Sexist Piggery Has Women's Section," *Globe and Mail* [Toronto], November 10, 1997, p. A14). For scholarly studies of genital names, see Martha Cornog's essays: "Tom, Dick and Hairy: Notes on Genital Pet Names," *Maledicta* 5, nos. 1&2 (1981): 31–40; "Naming Sexual Body Parts: Preliminary Patterns and Implications," *Journal of Sex Research* 22, no. 3 (1986): 393–98; "Language and Sex," in *Human Sexuality: An Encyclopedia*, ed. Vern L. Bullough and Bonnie Bullough (New York: Garland Publishing, 1994), pp. 341–47.

63. Alice Domurat Dreger, *Hermaphrodites and the Medical Invention of Sex* (Cambridge: Harvard University Press, 1998), p. 5.

64. Nussbaum is not only silly about sex, but constipated: "If I am lying around with my lover on the bed, and use his stomach as a pillow, there seems to be nothing at all baneful about this, *provided that* I do so with his consent" ("Objectification," p. 296; italics added). The concluding legalistic proviso applies, of all things, to being in bed with "my lover."

65. See my *Sexual Investigations*, p. 84–90.

66. Michael S. Kimmel, "Introduction: Guilty Pleasures—Pornography in Men's Lives," in *Men Confront Pornography*, ed. Michael S. Kimmel (New York: Crown Publishers, 1990), p. 9. For discussion of Kimmel's gripes about the self-objectification and phallocentrism of male masturbation, see my *Sexual Investigations*, pp. 93-96.

67. Lawrence, *Lady Chatterley's Lover*, pp. 212-13.

68. Ibid., pp. 196-97. See the passage quoted by Nussbaum, "Objectification," p. 302.

69. To the dismay of Alexander Portnoy. See Philip Roth,

Portnoy's Complaint (New York: Random House, 1969). For MacKinnon's version, see chap. 1, p. 17.

70. Lawrence, *Lady Chatterley's Lover*, p. 225.

71. Nussbaum is forever the optimist, but she might be right: "In Lawrence, being treated as a cunt is a permission to expand the sphere of one's activity and fulfillment" ("Objectification," p. 307). As the U.S. Army says to prospective recruits, in the spirit of John Stuart Mill, "Be All That You Can Be." (For Mill, see *On Liberty* [Indianapolis: Hackett, 1978], chap. 3.)

72. It was not Freud who voiced this memorable line, but Rudolf Chrobak, who was quoted by Freud in "On the History of the Psycho-Analytic Movement," in *The Standard Edition of the Complete Psychological Works of Sigmund Freud*, ed. and trans. James Strachey (London: Hogarth Press, 1953–74), vol. 14, pp. 14–15. See also Wilhelm Reich: "My contention is that . . . there is only one thing wrong with neurotic patients: the *lack of a full and repeated sexual satisfaction*" (*The Discovery of the Orgone. Vol. 1: The Function of the Orgasm* [New York: Noonday Press, 1961], p. 73, where Reich commends Chrobak). I think Reich is nearly right; his view fits nicely with my view, and Fred Berger's, that the human is nothing but the animal.

THREE

SLUTS, FACIALS, SHITTING

*I [Toby, a stallion] have to tell you something about Lily—
she's the mare . . . who grazes in the next pasture. She has a
yellow mane. . . . You may have no way to understand just
how wonderful a yellow mane is. Well, on Lily it's wonderful.
Sometimes at night she will slide along the fence and come
close to me, and she will sigh her warm breath on my nose,
and I will rub my head against her yellow mane, and the
smell will stay with me until morning. She also has a great
asshole. Oh, I forgot. You're human and you think that's
vulgar. Lily is about the closest thing to God that I've come
across.*

Steve Martin[1]

INDETERMINACY

Catharine MacKinnon's legal definition of pornography, part of the antipornography civil rights "Ordinance" she composed with Andrea Dworkin, is a grim catalogue of atrocities:

Pornography is the graphic sexually explicit subordination
of women, whether in pictures or in words, that also

91

includes one or more of the following: (i) women are presented dehumanized as sexual objects, things or commodi-
ties; or (ii) women are presented as sexual objects who enjoy
pain or humiliation; or (iii) women are presented as sexual
objects who experience sexual pleasure in being raped; or
(iv) women are presented as sexual objects tied up or cut up
or mutilated or bruised or physically hurt; or (v) women are
presented in postures of sexual submission, servility or display; or (vi) women's body parts—including but not limited
to vaginas, breasts, and buttocks—are exhibited, such that
women are reduced to those parts; or (vii) women are presented as whores by nature; or (viii) women are presented
being penetrated by objects or animals; or (ix) women are
presented in scenarios of degradation, injury, torture,
shown as filthy or inferior, bleeding, bruised, or hurt in a
context that makes these conditions sexual.[2]

Quite a frightening mouthful. Why should we take this
incendiary definition seriously? Dworkin and MacKinnon
offer this defense: "The Ordinance adopts a simple if novel
strategy for definition. It looks at the existing universe of the
pornography industry and simply describes what is there."[3]
That's a shock. Meant to apply to the whole domain, the definition is false, or at best overwhelmingly misleading. It
would have been more accurate for Dworkin and
MacKinnon to say that their definition "looks at a small seg-
ment of pornography and describes *that*." Either Dworkin
and MacKinnon do not know the variety of pornography in
the universe, or they do not care about its variety. Atrocity, on
their view, a priori and necessarily, pervades all available
sexual material, even the pictorials of *Playboy*.

Isn't the Dworkin-MacKinnon definition tendentious and
contentious? Not for them. "The definition is closed, concrete, and descriptive, not open-ended, conceptual, or
moral," they write.[4] But their definition must in large part be

"moral" or "conceptual," since it contains the notions "dehumanization" and "degradation." And in what possible sense is the definition "closed" and "concrete"? Speaking in broad strokes about "dehumanization," already an emotionally loaded word, the definition does not contain much concrete detail. In clause (v), for example, the definition does not specify exactly what bodily positions are "postures of sexual submission." Bending over might be a posture of sexual submission but, then again, it might be a command to plant an idolizing kiss. Hence clause (v) is indeterminate in its meaning, not "concrete." Heterosexual intercourse in the "doggie" position, or intercourse *a tergo*, might be seen as a submissive posture for a woman to assume, in agreement with those medieval Catholic ethicists who objected to this sexual position because it made animals out of humans and thereby degraded them.[5] Or maybe not; it is often a position merely used to provide variety or to allow the penis to enter more deeply and sensuously or at a different angle. Given this indeterminacy, in practice the definition leaves it up to the traditional and sexist notion of postures of sexual submission that would be employed by a jury of one's uneducated (OK, undereducated) peers. Since when are Dworkin and MacKinnon big on mass democracy? We might suspect that the Dworkin-MacKinnon definition of pornography goes beyond being merely indeterminate in its meaning and is actually an attempt of some feminists and their conservative supporters to smuggle into the civil law their own preferred notion of politically correct sexual positions. But such optimism would be hasty, for, if we are to take Dworkin at her word, *any* sexual position in which a man and a woman engage in coitus is one in which the woman is in a position of submission. Heterosexual coitus, she claims, makes a woman inferior: communicating to her cell by cell her own inferior status, impressing it on her, burning it into her by shoving it into her, over and over, pushing and thrusting until she gives in.[6]

More than being merely indeterminate or a proposal to make civilly liable the harmful dissemination of depictions of politically incorrect sex, the definition disguises a deeper, more nefarious, agenda, one that expresses pure contempt for any heterosexuality at all. It makes sense, then, that Dworkin and MacKinnon think that the innocuous centerfolds of *Playboy* are atrocious.

Feminist legal scholar Susan Easton asserts that the Dworkin-MacKinnon definition is basically fine:

The . . . Ordinance was criticised for its vagueness. Terms such as "sexual objectification," "degradation" and "subordination" . . . , it was argued, leave too much scope for judicial interpretation which could be exploited by the moral right and could be used against feminist and gay writers and publishers. . . . Clearly vagueness in drafting needs to be addressed carefully, but this is not an insuperable problem. It can be taken account of in considering similar legislation in the future.[7]

I do not understand why Easton is worried only about conservative prosecutors, juries, and judges employing the Ordinance against feminist and gay/lesbian material, that is, what is for her politically correct sexuality. Easton here fails to be an objective jurisprudentialist. The material of all sexual minorities, including sexually deviant male heterosexuals, is also endangered by the Ordinance. About that she is not worried, only that the Ordinance might be used against friends of its drafters, or its drafter herself.[8] Easton has flagrantly politicized the noble discipline of jurisprudence.

The important point here, however, is that it is sopho-
moric to think that a little tinkering with the Dworkin-
MacKinnon definition of pornography will do the trick.
Easton doesn't seem to have a clue about the extent of con-
testability and indeterminacy in the concepts used in the definition. Clause (viii), which mentions depictions in which
women are penetrated by "objects," is both vague and
curious. This odd clause does not have the nasty flavor that
the other clauses have; one wonders, then, why it is in the
definition at all. Wouldn't "being penetrated by animals"
have sufficed? (MacKinnon, we know, thinks that bestiality
images are degrading and brutal.) After all, some women
enjoy being penetrated by phallic objects, be they dildos,
vibrators, sausages, cucumbers, corn, squash, or extremely
thick or long penises. What Dworkin and MacKinnon might
mean—I suppose, in order to make their meaning reasonable—is that the woman is penetrated, and brutally so, by a
baseball bat or a broom handle. But such depictions are
already covered by clause (iv), which covers physical harm,
if not other clauses. Thus we have no way to explain the
mention of "objects" in clause (viii), except to assume that
Dworkin and MacKinnon really do mean that the dissemination of depictions of dildos and vegetables being introduced
into a woman's vagina or her anus or mouth is in fact made
actionable by the Ordinance. Then we realize what Dworkin
and MacKinnon are up to, not merely condemning brutality
but that which is for them obnoxiously deviant.[9] Clause (viii)
exposes MacKinnon's conservative card.[10] We do not know
for sure, however, that Dworkin and MacKinnon intend to
disparage depictions of vegetables entering a vagina. Nor do
we know that their words in themselves disparage such
depictions. This is why the conclusion that the clause is indeterminate is formidable, if not certain. To delete the vague
clause about "objects" altogether is one possible way to

tinker with and improve the definition. But then, to be consistent, we would have to scratch out all the other clauses as well, one by one, improving the definition by eliminating all its vagueness and indeterminacy. Or we could try to tighten up the clause about "objects," say, by specifying of what diameter an object must be (including a penis? a hand?) to fall within the meaning of the clause. That seems like an impossible mission. Nonetheless, MacKinnon and Dworkin should have been more specific in describing the content of sexual dehumanization, what counts as objectionably degrading sexual acts and depictions. But, as we shall see, their conservative political allies and feminist colleagues have not done a convincing job of filling in the details.

An older feminist criticism of pornography is that it portrays women in a dehumanizing way, in the sense that in pornographic images, as the philosopher Ann Garry writes, "the woman's purpose is to cater to male desires, to service the man or men. Her own pleasure is rarely emphasized for its own sake."[11] This criticism was false when it was voiced; the inference that in most pornography the woman's pleasure is rarely the center of attention could only have been based on a cursory look at the genre. Or maybe it was a mere knee-jerk repetition of a feminist stereotype of pornography. Yet this criticism was frequently belabored. The feminist writer Susan Griffin dramatically articulated it:

> [T]he pornographer's idea of his object's pleasure is to please him. She exists for no other purpose. . . . Throughout pornography, this image of a penis in a woman's mouth is among the most popular of images. And under this image we hear the pornographic voice whisper, "*She* exists for *his* pleasure."[12]

I really do wonder who the "we" are who hear that dim whisper coming from a polysemic image, other than Griffin.

That is, Griffin seems to be projecting into such pornographic images her own favored and feared reading and attributing that reading to its viewers. Or she is elevating her own reading into the one true, objective reading of the image. Griffin, however, is not satisfied with expounding this criticism, and forces pornography into a catch-22, for she also claims the opposite:

> So we see her beg for this pleasure, as if it were hers alone. One sees this image over and over in pornography—a woman driven to the point of madness out of the desire to put a man's penis in her mouth.[13]

Pornography dehumanizes women both by making them subservient to male desire (all the sexual pleasure is his) and by making women too desirous of their own sexual pleasure (all the sexual pleasure is hers). Perhaps that Griffin finds both messages in these pornographic depictions reveals to us her own dichotomous and ambivalent attitude toward heterosexual fellatio. But Griffin nevertheless was on to something that was overlooked by Garry: much pornography depicts women as motivated by sexual desire of their own and as sexually gluttonous.[14] On Griffin's view, women are depicted as dehumanized because they are shown, in the traditional social definition of these things, as sluts, as Judith Hill's mindless nymphomaniacs (see p. 59, above). The pornographic woman, an active seeker of her own sexual pleasure, initiates not "out of her own genuine affection"[15] (or her love), but out of her own corrupt randiness. Dworkin and MacKinnon agree: "[A]dult women are presented as children, fusing the vulnerability of a child with the sluttish eagerness to be fucked said to be natural to the female of every age."[16] But polysemicity intrudes: what appears to feminist-Augustinian viewers as sluttish behavior appears to liberal feminists in more wholesome terms, for example the ACLU lawyer Nadine Strossen: "Many sexual materials defy traditional stereotypes of . . . women . . . by depicting females as voluntarily, joyfully participating in sexual encounters with men."[17] What a clean mind such a viewer must have, or one relatively free of the traditional, conservative cultural meanings of sex.

Because pornographic images are polysemic, we can see the woman eagerly performing fellatio as submissively subservient solely to the man's desire, or as a sluttish glutton for her own pleasure, or as a woman enjoying sex without making excuses. Each of us should be able to imagine interpreting such a photograph in all three, if not more, ways. The fact that someone sees the active, promiscuous woman—either in pornography or in real life—predominantly as a slut tells us more about the viewer's values and sexual presuppositions, including the values of the legal or philosophical analyst, than about the photograph or sexual act itself. Linda Williams asks,

> What does it mean when in *Insatiable* . . . Marilyn Chambers's multiply orgasmic heroine cries out for "more, more, more," even though she has apparently had an enormous amount of sexual pleasure already? Is Chambers a modern-day Hera damning herself once again by letting out the quantitative secret of her ability to keep on enjoying?[18]

What Sphinxish secret do the critics of sluttish pornography fear is being spilled? Perhaps that women are as sexually greedy as men, despite the traditional belief or value to the contrary. Or that women are naturally, by their own imprisoning or constraining biology, sexually insatiable.[19] Or that in being portrayed in pornography as active seekers of their own pleasure, women are shown announcing to men, other

women, and the world that they are stupid enough to give it
away, to abandon their power and rights, that they are genuinely mindless. We must, it seems, object to sluttish pornography paternalistically, to protect women, universally and
essentially vulnerable, from being the victims of the truth of
their own base desires.[20] To do this, we poke out the eyes of
the male viewer of pornography or, equivalently, take away
his stash. We know that men, too, in pornography are "portrayed as socially nondiscriminating in their relentless pursuit of sexual gratifications."[21] Critics of pornography only
rarely raise an eyebrow at this male promiscuity. In saying
that the women are depicted as sluts, but not saying this
about men (but what word could they use?), these critics buy
into the traditional double standard of their home culture.
Their condemnation of the pornographic woman as a mindless slut is informed by the traditional sexist view of the sexually hungry or needy or aggressive woman, even if these
critics are "progressive" feminists. Alternatively, we could
refuse to see pornographic women as sluts at all, or we could
agree that women in pornography are portrayed as sluts, but
see this fact in a positive light, as undermining the misleading, chaste Mary model of women. Both moves buck
recent tradition. When Griffin and Dworkin and MacKinnon
see the pornographic woman as a slut, and proclaim her to be
that, they have not merely abandoned the fight against
sexual conservatives in the construction of meaning, they
have joined arm-in-arm with them and hence reinforce the
very meanings that they find outrageous.

Sharpening the Razor

A tripartite categorization of sexual materials has been
gaining in popularity. Although this approach is more

nuanced than Dworkin and MacKinnon's, who call the whole domain dehumanizing and degrading, the proposed distinctions seem scholastic and impotent. After dividing the universe of sexual material into two types of bad stuff, "sexually violent pornography" and "non-violent dehumanizing pornography," and the good or permissible stuff, "erotica," the social psychologist James Check approvingly quotes a Canadian judge who similarly divides sexual materials into these three groups: "In terms of operational definitions of these terms, Mr Justice Mel Shannon of the Alberta (Canada) Court of Queen's Bench had this to say after hearing various expert testimonies (including my own) in his 1985 Canadian obscenity ruling (*R. v. Wagner*, 1985; p. 331):

> In sexually explicit pornography that is . . . *degrading or dehumanizing*, men and women are often verbally abused and portrayed as having animal characteristics. Women, particularly, are deprived of unique human character or identity and are depicted as sexual playthings, hysterically and instantly responsive to male sexual demands. They worship male genitals and their own value depends on the quality of their genitals and breasts. . . .
>
> On the other hand, sexually explicit *erotica* portrays positive and affectionate human sexual interaction, between consenting individuals participating on a basis of equality. There is no aggression, force, rape, torture, verbal abuse or portrayal of humans as animals."[22]

Justice Shannon has constructed an empty dichotomy. In dehumanizing pornography, women do not have a "unique human character" and respond to sexual advances "instantly." So, they *are* unique in erotica and do not respond instantly, just because they are not engaged in animal-like sex or because they express affection? Hardly. Women can and do respond instantly and powerfully in all manner of context. Women who "make love" are no more unique than women who fuck. Women remain as fungible in "erotica" as they are in "dehumanizing pornography." Maybe that's why Dworkin and MacKinnon lump *Playboy* with all the other, brutal material. If so, their objection to pornography rests on its being objectifying, and they are right, all sexual images do objectify. This means, then, that their objection is to sex itself, because sex is by its nature objectifying.

The important point to be made here against Check and Shannon is that there is no *erotica*, plain and simple, in their sense: Whether a purportedly "affectionate" couple is seen as fucking like animals or "making love" depends on the viewer, not the content of the image. Roger Scruton acknowledges that the viewer of the image makes the difference, not the content of the image, but then misses a golden opportunity:

> [T]he distinction between the genuinely erotic and the licentious is a distinction not of *subject-matter*, but of perspective. The genuinely erotic work is one which invites the reader to re-create in imagination the first-person point of view of someone party to an erotic encounter. The pornographic work retains as a rule the third-person perspective of the voyeuristic observer.[23]

To the contrary, what we ordinarily call "pornography" as a rule allows, if not encourages, the identification of the viewer with the first-person perspective of the participants. How else does the male viewer looking at an image of a woman performing fellatio on a man's penis experience and respond with arousal to her doing the act, unless he identifies with and imagines her pleasure, her sensations, her desires, her lustful appetite, what is going on in her mind? Scruton's more sophisticated analysis still does not provide us with a distinction between the good stuff and the bad stuff. His neglecting to notice how much a role identification plays in his bad stuff tells us only that he is not a consumer of pornography and cannot (like many feminists) comprehend the mind of the consumer and the subtle interaction that occurs between his wishes and desires and the content of the image.

Dehumanizing pornography, on Check and Shannon's view, sounds just like loveless fucking. Hence, what they object to is what offends their sociologically ignorant, traditional moral sensibility. The pornographic woman is not, to her discredit, the faithful and happy housewife who "makes love" tenderly and only with her husband, or the devoted and loyal girlfriend who has a relationship of full equality with her socially and sexually conscious boyfriend. The woman in pornography, on their view, unlike any real woman, or unlike what women are supposed to do, may actually worship male genitals. (As Constance Chatterley might have admitted, when admiring Mellors's stiff prick, his organ has more immediacy and provides more sensuous pleasure than the Christian God.) And the woman's value lies in the superb quality of her sexual parts. Men are known to exclaim "Oh, God!" or "Oh, shit!" when inspecting an especially choice specimen of female vagina or asshole. (Horses, too, says Steve Martin.) Check and Shannon are no pagans, and would presumptuously extirpate these pagan impulses from human sexuality.

Shannon's charge that women in dehumanizing pornography are hysterical—Griffin's "madness"—shows that he has not thought very long or hard about pornography, too put off by its perceived dehumanizing character to be able to cogitate clearly about it. First, male arousal and pleasure can be exhibited easily in pornography, through erection and ejaculation. It is more difficult to show and see in pornography, as it is in real life, female arousal and pleasure. (Women thus have the skill, perhaps of some evolutionary significance or origin, of being able to fake it.) The frenzied activity of women in pornography is in part meant as a way of displaying, as unambiguously as possible, her arousal and pleasure; it is done theatrically, in an exaggerated fashion, to make the point less obscure. The male viewer can more easily respond with desire and arousal to, or identify with, her arousal when it is clearly depicted. Second, male viewers, some of whom have doubts about the attractiveness of their penises, can be reassured by the woman's abundant enjoyment of the organ, as she lavishes enthusiastic, lusty kisses on it instead of gagging or barfing. "[E]very little girl . . . sees it for the ugly pendulous thing it is. . . . [S]he forgives her lover his eccentric appendage rather as one might forgive a beautiful-ugly dog panting its devotion."[24] Shannon's reading of female sexual enjoyment, responsiveness, and assertiveness in pornography as *hysteria* seems to presuppose, in Victorian manner, that women's sexuality is suspicious. This prevents him from devising or harboring other ways to understand the pornographic woman's pleasure.

The *Final Report of the Attorney General's Commission on Pornography* also makes a tripartite division of sexual material, using "degrading" for the material that is neither violent nor erotica. Does the distinguished panel of commissioners fare any better in explaining the terrain? The *Final Report* states:

> An enormous amount of the most sexually explicit material available . . . is material that we would characterize as "degrading," the term we use to encompass the undeniably linked characteristics of degradation, domination, subordination, and humiliation. . . . [H]ere we are referring to material that . . . depicts people, usually women, as existing solely for the sexual satisfaction of others, usually men, or that depicts people, usually women, in decidedly subordinate roles in their sexual relations with others, or

that depicts people engaged in sexual practices that would
to most people be considered humiliating.[25]

The commission reverts to the older understanding of the
dehumanization of women in pornography that we found in
Garry and Griffin: Women "exist . . . solely for the sexual satisfaction of others." In the universe of the *Final Report*, the
sexually assertive pornographic woman does not engage in
these activities for her own selfish pleasure. In a footnote, the
Final Report quotes the social psychologist Dolf Zillmann,
who observes that in pornography women are portrayed as
"socially nondiscriminating nymphomaniacs." Zillmann's
insight doesn't make its way into the *Final Report*'s definition
of degrading pornography.[26] That is, there is no room in the
Final Report's categorization for the portrayal of women as
sexually selfish or as determined to get their own pleasure, as
much as they can, here and now.[27] If the pornographic or real
woman, as the *Report* has it, exists for the sake of satisfying
others, then she is being portrayed as generous, as caring for
and about the good of others. Is this falsehood, that women
are more sexually giving, more selflessly *agapic*, than they
really are, defamatory or degrading? Pornography is caught
in another catch-22: it degrades women by depicting them as
giving, and being deferential to the sexual needs or desires of
their male companions; and if it depicts them as taking,
instead, as motivated primarily by their own lust, it still
degrades them. (If giving to the other during sexual activity
is a paramount way of getting one's own pleasure, then
women are in all cases degradingly depicted as seekers of
only their own sexual pleasure.) Maybe the point is that men
and women in sex, and hence in pornography, should always
give and take equally. That's a vanilla definition of acceptable sex and acceptable sexual materials that misunderstands
eros, and it sets an unacceptably high standard for the quality

of relationships. Still, some equality already occurs in this "degrading" pornography. Both the man and the woman are satisfied, even if in the fantasy world of pornography she is often satisfied by doing the particular acts that satisfy him, or if their sexual tastes, be they perverted or ordinary, by some invisible sexual hand always tally with each other. (What would one expect from pornography created for men? Let women make their own pornography that panders to their fantasies.) In this sense, there is little difference between degrading pornography and the "non-degrading" material that the *Final Report* defines later, in which "the participants appear to be fully willing participants occupying substantially equal roles."[28] That "most people," according to the *Final Report*, find some of or all the acts that the woman performs for the man's sake, or for her own sake, "humiliating" and hence degrading, is too frivolous to be given any credit. Why should we coddle socially traditional notions of humiliation? The standard thought of "most people" is dumb and sexist, and is therefore a rather weak hook on which to hang "degrading," for purposes of either law or morality. (Most people think miscegenation is disgusting and degrading. Surely, that they think so means nothing.)

THE DETAIL DEVIL

In the introduction to her anthology *Making Violence Sexy*, the sociologist and antipornography activist Diana Russell tells her reader:

> Most of the chapters in this book will focus on *male heterosexual pornography,* which I define as *material created for heterosexual males that combines sex and/or the exposure of genitals with the abuse or degradation of females in a manner that appears*

to endorse, condone, or encourage such behavior. . . . Erotica refers to sexually suggestive or arousing material that is free of sexism, racism, and homophobia, and respectful of all human beings and animals portrayed.[29]

Russell belongs to the literal reading of pornography school. Given the problems in our (and his) knowing what the male viewer is inspecting in the image, what triggers his sexual arousal, what he is imagining while working over the surface content, it is thoughtless for Russell to talk confidently about pornography created for "heterosexual males" that involves the "degradation" of women. The surface content of this "heterosexual" pornography might be a woman on her knees performing fellatio between the thighs of a seated male. But what registers in the mind of the viewer, either consciously or unconsciously, might be (among other candidates) that *he* is on his knees performing the act, without any twinge of something degrading going on. Only the surface content is degrading to the woman, if even that; the meaning of the image for the viewer is something different, and has a neutral moral tone. And it is crude for Russell to call this material "male heterosexual pornography," for the same reason, that the viewer might use the image to fantasize about performing the fellatio he is witnessing the woman doing. Russell ignores the contribution of the viewer's wishes and desires that underlie the polysemicity of images. As a result, her blessing "erotica" is equally simplistic, for *any* depiction of a sexual act, including those that Russell would find "free of sexism," can generate the response in the viewer that the woman is degraded. The surface content of her erotica, as of all sexual images, is polysemic; and whether a depiction is free of sexism (and so forth) depends on the viewer, not the photograph. Consider a male viewer of a traditional cultural bent, a clone of Jerry Falwell, slobbering over a photograph of what Russell sees as a respectful couple engaged in loving, egalitarian sex. This guy whispers "slut" to himself, because the woman allowed herself to be photographed during a sexual act, because she is a participant, in his mind, in an abnormal sexual event, or because she enjoys sexual acts that nice girls shouldn't enjoy—because, in a word, the female model is engaged, for him, in religiously, morally, medically, or politically incorrect sexual behavior. If Russell wants to eliminate degrading pornography and produce only "erotica," she has to get rid of this guy, not the photographs or descriptions she finds objectionable, or she has to reeducate him. Connie Chatterley is, for this same viewer, a slut. His reading of D. H. Lawrence's *Lady Chatterley's Lover* is not without foundation. Is she or isn't she (really) a slut? Only her viewer knows. The bare description of her character and behavior doesn't know (or tell). Despite the firm embodiment of Lawrence's more pristine values in the text, this man can still see Connie as a slut, overriding the author's authority and intention. Indeed, where Lawrence went wrong was in venerating sluthood.[30]

Russell does supply specific examples, but the ones she selects to exhibit the degradation of women in pornography suggest that she has accepted traditional, sexually conservative notions of proper, nondegrading sex. "The requirement of nonsexism," writes Russell, "means that the following types of material qualify as pornography rather than erotica: sexually arousing images in which women are consistently shown naked while men are clothed or in which women's genitals are displayed but not men's."[31] It is degrading, for Russell, in both sex and depictions of sex, for men to be clothed while the woman is naked. I don't get it (and neither would people like Nadine Strossen). We could see acts or images of that sort as degrading to the woman, but no one is forced to. And if a single image of a sexual encounter between a clothed man and a naked women does not express her degradation, then Russell's "consistently" wouldn't necessarily make it otherwise. Seeing these images as expressing the degradation of the woman requires that the viewer, including the analyst (Russell), accepts certain social meanings that are imposed on the act or image. Here's a contrary example. The man fully dressed lounging about in a bar, watching a naked woman dance, is being cock teased; he might feel himself being humiliated and degraded, and he might very well be right. Or he might not. What about, for another example, the masturbation or fellatio that a woman does to a man when only his penis is uncovered, erection painfully sticking out between the zipper of his open fly, and she is fully dressed? Here the man is exposed and vulnerable; she is protected by her clothing. He could be seen as degraded, and so, alternatively or in addition, could she. But neither person needs to be seen that way. These examples muddy Russell's water. What Russell or her defender must do is to argue that some pornographic depictions are *intrinsically* degrading to women to the extent that the input of the viewer's fantasy makes no difference to the meaning of these images, or that certain sexual acts (other than violent rape, to make the argument interesting) are in themselves degrading. I doubt such a claim can be sustained, but Russell proffers it: "*Degrading* sexual behavior refers to sexual conduct that is humiliating, insulting, disrespectful, for example, urinating or defecating on a woman, ejaculating in her face."[32] Note that Russell's objection is not to some probable harmfulness of the activity or the absence of consent, but to its purely "degrading" nature, regardless of context, what the participants believe they are doing, and how they evaluate its worth.

Depositing bodily substances on a woman—the ejaculate, urine, feces—is, for Russell, a candidate for a sexual act that is intrinsically degrading, or degrading in itself. Catherine

Itzin, another antipornography feminist, apparently agrees with some of this: "ejaculation into the face of a woman is arguably dehumanising."[33] But she doesn't explain herself. Is semen disgusting in itself, the sort of stuff that women by their nature find revolting? I am not convinced. The facial ejaculation is, arguably, not dehumanizing at all, but, perhaps, a profoundly intimate and bonding sexual act. Which it is depends not on the act itself but on its context, its setting, and how the participants and the viewers of images evaluate it. Strossen, the liberal feminist defender of pornography, sees ejaculatory sexual activity as wholesome:

> Although procensorship feminists routinely cite these as archetypal images of female degradation [men ejaculating on women], this characterization is . . . oversimplified. . . . Many women viewers may be particularly interested in seeing come shots because men's ejaculations are usually hidden from them, occurring inside the woman's own body. . . . [T]he come-shot can be interpreted in an almost romantic way: the woman wishes to share, as much as possible, in her lover's orgasm.[34]

Where better to share the ejaculate and thereby enhance his pleasure, and how more effective for her to show her acceptance of him and his fluids, than by receiving the ejaculate in the mouth or on the face—the seat of the soul? Men need reassurance, and ejaculatory pornography does this, for their "sexuality, embodied in an organ reminiscent of a slug that emits viscous ooze, makes every man, in men's view, unimaginable to women except as a source of horror, a monster."[35] Whether facial ejaculation is degrading, and only or precisely that, is contentious, and that upsets the attempt (e.g., Russell's) to use some content-based, objective notion of sexual degradation for the law as well as in morality. How the sides are drawn seems to depend on sexual and political philosophy, with antipornography feminists siding with sexual conservatives against an inglorious group of sexual liberals, hedonists, anarchists, and nihilists—dirty old men, perverts, one and all. Some studies tell us that most women (80 percent) do not find performing fellatio "very appealing"[36]—perhaps because there is the danger of squirting semen. Almost naturally, women will find images of heterosexual fellatio threatening and degrading, since they find the act, even or especially when they do it out of consideration or duty, distasteful. No wonder, then, that heterosexual fellatio and facial ejaculations are depicted in pornography. But this pornographic fellatio may not be as much about a man's degrading a woman as it is about his getting a yearned-for, and perhaps illusory, consolation. Perusing this pornography might very well make some men critical of some of their lovers (or wives), and perhaps justifiably so. For the same studies reveal that women surely like *receiving* oral sex from their men, at the same time that they don't much enjoy *giving* it.[37]

THE NITTY GRITTY

Now to dispose of the urine and fecal dumping objection. Didn't you enjoy the stuff when you were a kid? What happened to you, since that time? You were royally scrutinized and socialized, by the same society that gave you sexism, homophobia, and other antisexualisms, not to mention racism, antimiscegenation, and agism, not a society to have faith in when fashioning a notion of sexual degradation. Along the way, you repressed the infantile links in Freud's equation among feces, gift, penis, baby.[38] "The excremental is all too intimately and inseparably bound up with the sexual; the position of the genitals—*inter urinas et faeces*—remains the decisive and unchangeable factor."[39] Or, as William Butler Yeats put it, more succinctly, "Love has pitched his mansion in the place of excrement."[40] Defecation and urination are degrading?—only by thinking sexuality has nothing to do with our histories, with the grounding and origin of our adult sexuality in our infantile bodies and drives. The sharing of urine and feces sexually might be a sign of deep love and communion, the perfect, ultimate physical intimacy between lovers.[41] Alternatively, or in addition, sexual defecation and urination might simply signify an openness to exploring the full inventory of potential bodily pleasures in sex. If, or when, sharing excrement is infinitely intimate— perhaps exactly because it is the disgusting exchange par excellence—then images of defecation would, on Russell's own definition, be erotica, not pornography. If so, Russell's definitions do not achieve for her what she wanted, a distinction between permissible, unobjectionable sexual material and activities and those images and acts that are intolerable. Russell's monodimensional appreciation of the sexual, reflected in her dry and lifeless definitions, are insensitive to the meanings that participants give to their sexual acts. Some gay men, we know, are into "scat," for either the love and intimacy or the sheer raunchy pleasure of it, but maybe, for Russell, that which is objectionable about heterosexual scat games does not apply to homosexual scat games. Try this: dumping doesn't have the same social meaning; or homosexual couplings are more likely to be free of obnoxious power relations.

The ultimate physical union is not, as the philosopher Vincent Punzo would have it, heterosexual coitus, in which a man "has literally entered" a woman. "A man and a woman engaging in sexual intercourse have united themselves as intimately and as totally as is physically possible for two human beings,"[42] says Punzo. Similarly, as the theologian

Gilbert Meilaender affirms, heterosexual coitus is "the act in which human beings are present most fully and give themselves most completely to another."[43] No, and only the sexually naive would think so. The intimacy of a sexual act might very well vary, for example, directly with its grossness. Oral sex, then, might foster intimacy through the contrast between the high symbolism of the face of one person and the low symbolism of the genitals and ass of the other person, when the face and crotch come into contact with each other. Heterosexual coitus is often one of the least intimate, and most sterile, sexual acts in which a couple can engage; the detached and far away genitals merely mumble to each other, and do not always fit together harmoniously. Heterosexual coitus can be, as my students readily agree, much less intimate than french kissing, oral sex (with all its vaginal and penile fluids), and vaginal and anal fistfucking.[44] Indeed, much of the intimacy in heterosexual coitus is provided by the insistent kissing and tongue sucking that can occur during genital congress, not by the genital congress itself.[45] The technical female virgin, who has done everything sexual under the sun with her casual partners except vaginal intercourse, has not saved the most intimate sexual activity for her husband. She already lost it, or has given it away, during her first drunken french kiss, sucking the bacteriologically filthy tongue of a guy she just met in a bar. If the technical virgin thinks that heterosexual coitus is worth saving for her husband, it must be for some reason other than its intimacy. "I saved *this* for *you*, my darling husband" really means, "Now, with your economic support and the social benediction of legal matrimony, I do not have to worry about getting pregnant." Then she withholds from her proper husband all the intimate anal intercourse she endured for the sake of pleasing her casual lovers.

If "excretion is the final 'no' to all our transcendental illusions,"[46] if defecation flawlessly demonstrates to us our fundamentally infantile, asocial nature, and if shitting makes us realize that we are mere animals, it is understandable that, in our attempt to maintain the illusion that humans are metaphysically or spiritually special, we condemn the sexual interest in excretion and the anus, back that up with social sanctions, and philosophize how degrading it is. The *New Yorker* columnist Nicholas Lemann's perspective on these things is good evidence that the powers have done their job well. Lemann complains with equal outrage that one prostitute in a brothel in New Orleans's old Storyville district had to play bathroom games with a patron, while another prostitute had her nipples and clitoris bitten off by another patron—as if these two incidents were on a par among atrocities.[47] Given the insanity and depravity of the second incident, Lemann's combining it with the first in making his point about the revolting treatment of prostitutes is goofy.

About the anus and its product, D. H. Lawrence resisted sexual prejudice, while dismissing Jonathan Swift's sarcasm about the sexual unattractiveness of the woman (one's spouse, for example) who is known to defecate:[48]

> [Mellors] watched the beautiful curving drop of [Connie's] haunches. That fascinated him to-day. How it sloped with a rich down-slope to the heavy roundness of her buttocks! And in between, folded in the secret warmth, the secret entrances!
>
> He stroked her tail with his hand, long and subtly taking in the curves and the globe-fulness.
>
> "Tha's got such a nice tail on thee," he said. . . . "Tha's got the nicest arse of anybody. It's the nicest, nicest woman's arse as is! . . . It's a bottom as could hold the world up, it is."
>
> All the while he spoke he exquisitely stroked the rounded tail, till it seemed as if a slippery sort of fire came from it into his hands. And his finger-tips touched the two

secret openings to her body, time after time, with a soft little brush of fire.

"An' if tha shits an' if tha pisses, I'm glad. I don't want a woman as couldna shit nor piss."

Connie could not help a sudden snort of astonished laughter, but he went on unmoved.

"Tha'rt real, tha art! Tha'rt real, even a bit of a bitch. Here tha shits an' here tha pisses: an' I lay my hand on 'em both an' like thee for it. I like thee for it. Tha's got a proper, woman's arse, proud of itself. It's none ashamed of itself, this isna."

He laid his hand close and firm over her secret places, in a kind of close greeting.

"I like it," he said. "I like it! An' if I only lived ten minutes, an' stroked thy arse an' got to know it, I should reckon I'd lived *one* life, see ter!"[49]

There is more going on in this passage than Lawrence's philosophizing about the acceptance of the body's waste materials. The passage exhibits further the sexual objectification in the relationship between Oliver Mellors and Connie Chatterley. Mellors's remark, "Tha's got the nicest arse of anybody. It's the nicest, nicest woman's arse as is!" is no mere piece of flattery to Connie meant to assuage her doubts about her body, but a statement of a central theme in his sexual interest in her and her sexual interest in him: "if I only lived ten minutes, an' stroked thy arse an' got to know it, I should reckon I'd lived *one* life, see ter!" Like the dancer Sky and her audience at Onyx, Connie and Mellors are a perfectly complementary sexual couple: Mellors is an ass man, and Connie is proud of her ass. He objectifies it, and she is tickled pink that he does so.[50] Mellors's sexual admiration of Connie's ass proceeds, as the logic of such desire often does, to her ass's hole and its product. (Lawrence pretends that the Lady and Mellors are not mackerel, and that Mellors will never get bored with her ass.)

While we're on the anal orifice, let's examine Catherine Itzin's discussion of heterosexual anal intercourse and its pornographic depiction:

> The material depicting heterosexual buggery as consensual is . . . problematic. Anal intercourse is the standard sexual practice between gay males who each have the same social and sexual power status. This is not true of heterosexual relationships: in which the anus is not the standard orifice of intercourse and in which the participants do not enjoy the same social and sexual status. The extent to which anal sex is a consensual act for women must be questioned and consideration given in this, as in other contexts, to the extent to which this pornography operates to impose male sexual dominance and female subordination to sexual acts which are dehumanising for women.[51]

Itzin is extremely murky. Her objection to heterosexual anal intercourse and its depiction in pornography seems to rest on two criteria: (1) the anus is not the "standard" orifice for "intercourse" among heterosexuals, and (2) women and men are not "social and sexual" equals. Gay male anal coitus, by contrast, is unobjectionable because it passes both tests: (1) anal intercourse is their "standard" act, and (2) gay men have the "same" social and sexual power status. Oh? There are wealthy gays and poor gays, gays with respectable positions and those who bounce around, handsome gays and ugly gays, macho gays and effeminate gays, old gays and young gays, dull ones and those with sparkling personalities. Itzin's argument seems not to work, on the score that not all gay males have the same social and sexual status. Perhaps, then, gay male anal intercourse is unobjectionable exactly because it passes one test: the anus is the gay male's standard orifice. But even this is questionable. Given the gay male interest in fellatio, their standard orifice (if such a concept makes any sense at all) may well be the mouth.[52]

But even if gay male anal intercourse is unobjectionable because the anus is the standard orifice of the gay male, can it be maintained that heterosexual anal intercourse is objectionable, degrading to a woman, because a female's anus is not her standard orifice? Itzin, unfortunately, does not say whether she means "standard orifice" normatively (what people ought or ought not to do) or descriptively (what people in fact do or do not do). Suppose that Itzin means "standard" descriptively: heterosexuals do not engage in anal intercourse nearly as frequently as they engage in vaginal intercourse. What does that fact contribute to Itzin's thesis that the act is degrading to women? Merely being statistically unusual cannot be that in virtue of which a sexual act is degrading. What if heterosexuals did it more often than they do—would that tend to make it, for Itzin, less objectionable? My guess is that it would not. Itzin would still claim that women's participation in the act is objectionable because women are not the "social and sexual" equals of men. If so, Itzin's objection to heterosexual anal intercourse rests only on condition (2). Her objection to it is just a variant of the "women cannot consent to (any hetero-) sex in patriarchy" view, as in MacKinnon's outrageous claim, "Few women are in a position to refuse unwanted sexual initiatives" from men.[53] Itzin's objection is not to heterosexual anal intercourse, but to any heterosexual sex that occurs in the patriarchy.

Itzin's line, that gay men share with each other the same social and sexual power status, would seem reasonable only to one who has, under the influence of a totalizing political theory, abstracted from the particular details of persons' lives. Itzin does the same thing—raises the group to the level of an absolute analytic category, downplaying the features of distinct individuals—when she doubts whether women can or do consent to heterosexual anal intercourse. Under the sway of feminist political theory, Itzin forgets, ironically, to examine the particular details of women's lives, the circumstances in which they agree to anal intercourse, and the sometimes well-thought-out reasons they might have to do so, in addition to their liking or even craving it: to stay a vaginal virgin, to avoid pregnancy, to sidestep the messiness of vaginal sex during menstruation, or to please her doting, respectful male lover (some exist). Some women have even been known to initiate anal intercourse out of their own genuine desire and affection.[54] Itzin, for some reason, assumes that the women we know well are never autonomous actors, that they are always forced into anal intercourse by sexually greedy and pushy men. Robin Morgan, the feminist writer, is similarly suspicious, blaming pornography for men's rudeness:

> [H]ow to chart the pressure sensed by women from their boyfriends or husbands to perform sexually in ever more objectified . . . fashion as urged by pornography. . . ? How to connect the rise of articles in journals aimed at educated, liberal audiences—articles extolling the virtues of anal intercourse, "fistfucking," and other "kinky freedoms"?[55]

But it is scurrilous to assume, because our society places some excessive burdens and restraints on women, that women are by-and-large incapable of significantly autonomous decision and action. There are cases, and there are cases, and we might want to argue the details of each case. But to do so is to investigate the particulars of human relationships between women and men; it is to refuse to understand them by applying a strict and tidy formula of the "social and sexual" inequality of men and women, or of group male dominance and group female submission. Anyone who thinks that women cannot or do not consent to anal intercourse with men is not only sexually naive; he or she, driven by barren academic ideology, has no feel for life.

Here's more dryness. For Martha Nussbaum, the sexual activity of Mellors and Constance in *Lady Chatterley's Lover* occurs "in a context of mutual respect and rough social equality." She explains: "I mean here to say that a working-class man in England of that time is roughly comparable in social power to an upper-class woman."[56] What a crude unil-luminating calculus of interpersonal power. It would be better to admit that it is so "rough" as to be senseless, since it is glaringly insensitive to the psychological dynamics between two particular persons, which cannot be read straight off from their socioeconomic status and gender. The lower-class, uneducated, black, working woman, on a Nuss-baumian calculus, has little social power compared with the upper-class, white, professional male; yet, were these two to meet we have no way to predict, merely knowing these char-acteristics, which person, in any relationship that might ensue, would have the psychological upper hand. We would have to know features of their individual personalities, fea-tures that are not included in a Nussbaumian calculus.

But see Itzin's last sentence. She seems to mean that het-erosexual anal intercourse is *inherently* "dehumanising" for women—perhaps because it is not, in a *normative* sense, "standard." She does not seem to mean here that the act is "dehumanising" *because* it is forced on women who are unable to refuse, although that claim would fit nicely with "no woman can consent to heterosex in patriarchy." Perhaps Itzin's objection to heterosexual anal intercourse, then, is that it is inherently dehumanizing and, to boot, forced on frail women, who are underempowered. Even if the act were fully consensual, then, it could not be redeemed; the lack of the ability of women to consent to the act makes a dehumanizing act even worse. The act is not dehumanizing for gay men, by contrast, because it is normatively proper for them, given their sexual nature, and they don't have to worry, in Itzin's worldview, that it might be objectionable, apart from its nature, in virtue of a failure of the genuine consent of some of the participants. I have doubts. The penis of the penetrating male in homosexual anal intercourse often becomes coated with feces. Why doesn't Itzin see that as degrading to gay males? Not only to them, but also to the male penetrator in heterosexual anal intercourse? The woman is dumping her shit on his prized penis, the center of his ego—fairly good revenge against his "forcing" her, by his social and sexual superiority, to undergo such a disgusting act. Maybe we should be concerned that heterosexual anal intercourse is intrinsically degrading to the man, not to the woman. To say that the anus is not the normatively standard orifice for women is close to reverting to a Thomistic natural-law understanding of the sexual body: women were designed, or are supposed, to take the penis vaginally, not anally. (Itzin's Thomism is queer; it has always been the gay male anus that has been condemned as an organ for intercourse.) Of course, lesbians, who are always of the same social and sexual status, have vaginas, a woman's "standard orifice," and so never play around with their nonstandard anuses. Right? Itzin's sexual philosophy is applied incoherently: gay men who engage in anal intercourse escape the excoriation Itzin levels at heterosexual men. Whence, theoretically, Itzin's double standard in which gay anal intercourse, an act that can surely embody the power relations of fucker-fuckee if heterosexual anal intercourse does, is unobjectionable? No matter. Homosexuals are, as a group, politically correct and gay men as a group are, in Itzin's eyes, political allies.

The notion that heterosexual anal intercourse is "dehumanising" for women is a blunder. In Itzin's critique of pornography it amounts to an imposition of her own sexually conservative sense of sexual correctness. In contrast to Steve Martin's equine sexual philosophy (see the epigraph), feminists and sexual conservatives seem united in their determination to de-position the anus. "Pornography is a medical . . . problem because so much of it teaches false, misleading, and even dangerous information about human sexuality," claims Park Elliott Dietz, M.D., M.P.H., Ph.D., one of the conservative members of the Meese Commission. To provide one example of this kind of dangerously false information, Dietz writes: "A person who learned about sexuality [from pornography] . . . would be a person . . . who had learned that the anus was a genital to be licked."[57] Dietz suggests that in order to counter the false information contained in pornography, "the most straightforward remedy would be to provide factually accurate information on human sexuality to people."[58] But it is clear, I think, that Dietz's rejection of anilingis and anal intercourse rests primarily on his moral and religious values, not his medical "facts." For example:

I . . . have no hesitation in condemning nearly every specimen of pornography that we have examined in the course of our deliberations as tasteless, offensive, lewd, and indecent. According to my values, these materials are themselves immoral, and to the extent that they encourage immoral behavior they exert a corrupting influence on the family and on the moral fabric of society. . . . Pornography is but one of the many causes of immorality and but one of its manifestations. Nonetheless, a great deal of contemporary pornography constitutes an offense against human dignity and decency.[59]

Maybe what people really need to be taught is that the anus is indeed a source of sexual pleasure, both to the licker and the lickee, and that anal sexual acts need not be any more unhygienic than other sexual activities like deep kissing and cunnilingus. The pornography to which Dietz objects congenially provides images of daring, unconventional sex.[60] Of course, being sexually ambitious enough to explore the anus means becoming more like a horse, which reduction to the subhuman both the conservatives and the feminist daughters of Augustine fear. (That's queer: the horse is a noble animal.) Dietz would like to ensure that we do not have models of daring sex. We are not to be provoked to be ambitious. Seeing a zipless fuck, or reading about it,[61] we can overcome sexual naïveté, we might try things, experimenting with something, that turns out to be eye-opening and of earth-shattering significance—an epiphany. We might even find that we like, or are transported to heaven by, licking the anus of a person whom we met less than five minutes ago.[62] Dietz could just as easily condemn those misleading, false, and dangerously romantic Hollywood movies and television programs in which, unrealistically but usually, Love prevails over Hate and the Good is victorious over the Bad. While he is at it, he should condemn his own happy illusions of Christianity, including its misleading, false, and dangerous promise of everlasting life and bliss in the bosom of the Lord.

It is worthwhile to quote Dietz's descriptive summary of pornography in toto; his qualms about anilingis and scatology appear right at the end, as a fitting culmination of his inventory of sexual monstrosities:

A person who learned about human sexuality in the "adults only" pornography outlets of America would be a person who had never conceived of a man and a woman marrying or even falling in love before having intercourse, who had never conceived of two people making love in privacy without guilt or fear of discovery, who had never conceived of tender foreplay, who had never conceived of vaginal intercourse with ejaculation during intromission, and who had never conceived of procreation as a purpose of sexual union. Instead, such a person would be one who had learned that sex at home meant sex with one's children, stepchildren, parents, stepparents, siblings, cousins, nephews, nieces, aunts, uncles, and pets, and with neighbors, milkmen, plumbers, salesmen, burglars, and peepers, who had learned that people take off their clothes and have sex within the first five minutes of meeting one another, who had learned to misjudge the percentage of women who prepare for sex by shaving their pubic hair, having their breasts, buttocks, or legs tattooed, having their nipples or labia pierced, or donning leather, latex, rubber, or child-like costumes, who had learned to misjudge the proportion of men who prepare for sex by having their genitals or nipples pierced, wearing women's clothing, or growing breasts, who had learned that about one out of every five sexual encounters involves spanking, whipping, fighting, wrestling, tying, chaining, gagging, or torture, who had learned that more than one in ten sexual acts involves a party of more than two, who had learned that the purpose of ejaculation is that of soiling the mouths, faces, breasts, abdomens, backs, and food at which it is always aimed, who had learned that body cavities were designed for the insertion of foreign objects, who had learned that the anus was a genital to be licked and penetrated, who had learned that urine and excrement are erotic materials.[63]

In this and other passages, Dietz's conservative derogation of the interests of sexual minorities, including gays and lesbians, and his preference for the vanilla procreational sex of a married couple in the family unit, shine brightly.[64] Given these commitments, no one would ever expect feminist antipornographers to look favorably upon Dietz's diatribe. But they have. Jeanne Barkey and J. Koplin are members of the Minneapolis group Organizing Against Pornography, the organization that published Andrea Dworkin and Catharine MacKinnon's book *Pornography and Civil Rights: A New Day for Women's Equality*. In an essay they wrote that appears in the feminist antipornography collection edited by Catherine Itzin (*Pornography: Women, Violence and Civil Liberties*), Barkey and Koplin respectfully say:

> In a statement to the US Commission on Pornography, Park Elliott Dietz, professor of law, behavioural medicine and psychiatry at the University of Virginia and one of the authors of the research, summed up the messages of the materials surveyed and described what someone seeing it would have learned from it.[65]

Then Barkey and Koplin quote the entire inventory passage. The authors present Dietz's observations sympathetically, with approval, not bothering to mention that Dietz's sexual and family values are also antilesbian if not also sexist and patriarchal. Surely there is enough in the rest of Dietz's commission statement to give them pause, if not to frighten them. Here we have a case of antipornography feminists blindly lining up with antipornography conservatives, in an attempt to gain rhetorical advantage from Dietz's exposé of the horrors of pornography.[66] Of course, the group Organizing Against Pornography might not be a conservative association of right-wing women masquerading as feminists, but a feminist organization hiding its profoundly conservative aspirations. Same difference.

RACIAL MATTERS

Consider another image, a pornographic photograph of a black man and a white woman. Maybe she is sucking his cock, maybe they are fucking while she sucks his tongue, or maybe he is plunging his penis into her rectum. By a Nussbaumian calculus of power, the black man and the white woman are social and sexual equals: his superior maleness is offset by his blackness, her superior whiteness is offset by her being a mere female. But by society's traditional standards, or looking at it through that perspective, this sexual event and its depiction are degrading to the woman. Why is interracial sex of this sort never mentioned by feminists as an example of sex that is degrading to women? What *is* mentioned is anal intercourse, ejaculating on a woman's face, defecation, and, in MacKinnon's ordinance, inserting objects into a woman's vagina and sexual acts between women and animals. Leftist feminists (conservatives, too, for their own reasons) do not want to be accused of racism for claiming that interracial sexual events, with the white woman being fucked, or performing fellatio to completion, are degrading to the woman. That would court bad press. Being "progressives" and critical of social sexism, feminists do not want to invite being accused of buying into this traditional social standard of what is degrading to women. But they *do* buy into these traditional standards of degradation nonetheless, attributing to them an ontological status and power they do not have, regarding the acts they have opportunistically chosen to condemn publicly. These feminists embrace, albeit inconsistently, a conservative social constructionism. Precisely the society that through its construction of meanings says that the female fellator is a slut is the same one that constructed the meaning of interracial sex as degrading to its white female participant. In embracing the slut meaning, these feminists support that construction, and in supporting that construction they must also be, in effect even if not in intention, supporting the social construction of the meaning of interracial sex. Why not criticize all these constructed meanings, and their underlying social standards of degradation, instead of insisting that they determine the meaning of pornography? That would entail acknowledging, in agree-

ment with the principle of polysemicity, that social definitions are not hegemonic, that individual viewers are able to
override these messages. But then these feminists would be
conceding that their talk of the massive degradation of
women in pornography has been overblown.

It has been argued by feminist scholars, often convinc-
ingly, that mainstream (white, Western, male) social science
is biased, in part because it misrepresents or ignores the
experiences of women. Misconstruing or ignoring the experiences of the other sex (or gender) is not, however, restricted
to mainstream scholarship. Feminist (women) scholars have
also overlooked, trivialized, and twisted the experiences of
men (if not also of women). They talk about the minds of
men as if they knew them well. But they only think they
know them. They make it up. In effect, they deny the existence of men by ignoring men's experiences. We have seen
this before, in, for example, MacKinnon's pretending to read
the minds of men who buy and use pornography. Consider,
now, Laurie Shrage on men's tastes in prostitution, about
which Shrage proposes to solve a puzzle:

> A peculiar feature of prostitution—historically and cultur-
> ally—is the propensity of customers to cross national and
> ethnic boundaries to purchase sex. Given the social and
> legal barriers that are often erected to prevent racial, ethnic,
> and national "mixing," the popularity of cross-racial and
> cross-national prostitution is perplexing. . . . [W]hat
> explains the popularity of cross-racial and cross-national
> mixing in the sex industry, when such mixing is discour-
> aged in other domains of our social life?[67]

I don't see what is "peculiar" and "perplexing": Society
establishes barriers to all sorts of things, barriers that are routinely ignored. To find a problem in men's violating ethnic
boundaries in prostitution, one must assume that the barriers

are accepted, that they are taken seriously (by people other than Shrage), and that they have significant power to affect behavior. Almost every legal jurisdiction has laws and criminal penalties, and other forms of social condemnation, regarding prostitution, yet it flourishes. The barriers are routinely ignored. There are social barriers, laws or regulatory customs, against passing gas in public, cheating on taxes, adultery, and fellatio (ad infinitum) that are routinely ignored. What is so surprising? What is there to be "perplexed" about? Maybe there is no social prohibition against these things at all: the fact that much prostitution (tax cheating, adultery, farting, fellatio) exists gives the lie to the idea that society disapproves. Who is this "society," if not the persons who engage in cheating on taxes, adultery, farting, fellatio, prostitution? Maybe the barriers, whatever they are, *are* working: there would be more tax cheating, adultery, farting, fellatio, and interracial prostitution without them. But we don't know any such thing. Shrage pretends to know it; her claim, construed reasonably, is that there is more interracial mixing in prostitution than would be expected, given the social prohibitions. How many men, or what percent, engage in interracial mixing in prostitution? Is there more mixing than nonmixing, or vice versa? Shrage's use of "propensity" and "popularity" is appropriately vague. A philosopher, Shrage is doing sociology without the sociologist's empirical techniques. She provides no data to be explained.

There is no "perplexing" problem also because there is an abundance of plausible and obvious explanations why men cross racial "boundaries" in the pursuit of sex. If some customers violate what they take to be a social prohibition against interracial mixing, they might do so *because*, in their minds, that prohibition exists. Anyone with kids should know this, or anyone who recalls the story of Pandora and her box or the Adam and Eve myth. And the Wife of Bath is there to remind us, with her pointed and apropos example about the kind of men that women adore:

> I think I loved him best, I'll tell no lie.
> He was disdainful in his love, that's why.
> We women have a curious fantasy
> In such affairs, or so its seems to me.
> When something's difficult, or can't be had,
> We crave and cry for it all day like mad.
> Forbid a thing, we pine for it all night,
> Press fast upon us and we take to flight;
> We use disdain in offering our wares.[68]

Alternatively, for some men the appeal of prostitution, as in sexual matters generally, might be the promise of variety. Maybe whores of certain ethnicities are more talented, more experienced, less inhibited, taste better—or just different. I suspect that the supply of prostitution is the issue here, not, as in Shrage's statement of the problem, men's demand: it is a question of economics and demographics. Prostitutes of certain ethnicities might be more plentiful, less expensive, easier to locate, easier to purchase. It is wrongheaded to look for one determining reason why men who visit prostitutes ignore (or don't even think about) social prohibitions against interracial mixing. There is a multiplicity of reasons, just as there is a multiplicity of men. This brings us to the major flaw in Shrage's speculations. Why doesn't she *ask* men why they like, sometimes, prostitutes of a different race or nationality? Shrage blissfully proceeds to her dramatic and slanderous conclusions about men in the same way that mainstream social science was supposed to have proceeded to its nasty conclusions about women. Why does Shrage attempt to answer an empirical question about men from her philosopher's armchair?[69] Men, for the solipsistic Shrage, do not exist. The writer Daphne Merkin extracts from the feminism of Betty Friedan this methodology: "What do women want? Ask them one at a time."[70] The methodology of asking them one at a time would seem equally to illuminate the hearts of men.

In the absence of asking men about their reasons ("What do you men want?"), the result—Shrage's proposed solution to the puzzle—is bound to be infected, as are MacKinnon's writings, by a woman's projection, her immodest attempt to read the minds of men, and by her philosophical and political commitments. To wit:

> the sexual fantasy that propels the customer to the Asian prostitute is laden with political meaning. . . . [J]ohns who cross national and racial barriers for Asian prostitutes are typically acting upon principles that position easterners as inferior to westerners.[71]

Shrage presumes to know men's "sexual fantasy" about sex with Asian whores. The explanation Shrage concocts is "political": white Western men "typically" see Asians and Asian women as inferior. That's news to me. I've always had the fondest, yearning regard for those beauties (Korean, Japanese, Vietnamese, Chinese, Thai—let's reject Shrage's homogenizing "Asian"), and never for a second have I thought of them as inferior to me or to anyone else. Maybe Shrage, a white Western woman and proud of it, has internalized some traditional social standard that places Asian women below white Western women, and then attributes this nonsense to the men who seek Asian whores. This is similar to the way Russell and Itzin do not merely report social standards of sexual degradation but accept them. And why does Shrage write that men are *propelled* to Asian whores?—as if these men have a deep need to visit inferiors. Men go to Asian whores, they are propelled, *because*, for Shrage, they see Easterners as inferior. I don't see the sense in the explanation.

Why would men be driven to engage in sex with those women who, on Shrage's view, they see as inferiors (instead of, say, trying to degrade someone seen as superior or worth degrading—as in *Hustler*, the upper-class, spoiled rotten, bitchy, snotty white woman)? These men, ignoring the risk of being contaminated by having sexual contact with inferiors, must be reckless or masochistic, or both. Or they simply do not believe that they are in danger of being contaminated. That is, we could just as easily, and probably more accurately, say that men who seek Asian or Asian American whores are precisely the ones who do *not* accept the Western social idea (if it even exists) that Easterners are inferior: their going to Asian whores is the proof that they think Asian hookers as good as, or better than, anyone else. Shrage cannot know, without talking with men, whether those who visit Asian hookers think of these women as inferior and visit them for that reason or, instead, visit them because they think of them as equals or as superior (or never even consider the question). Given this weakness in her "social analysis" (not philosophy), Shrage should refrain from writing with such confidence and arrogance, or at all, about these matters, about men.

Shrage continues in the same fashion when she turns her attention to men who visit black prostitutes:

> the popularity of visiting black prostitutes may derive less from socially constructed sexual fantasies and more from socially constructed contempt. Seen as less than fully human on two counts—both by race and by sex—black wom[e]n are regarded as inherently degraded, and thus the appropriate partners for degrading sex.[72]

Shrage focuses, once again, on male demand instead of female supply: the "popularity" (higher than expected incidence?) of white men's having sex with black prostitutes, I think, might have more to do with the economic position of black women than with men's perplexing willingness to violate social rules and cross ethnic boundaries. Again, Shrage attributes certain beliefs and motives to the men who seek black prostitutes: black whores are seen as "inherently" degraded, being less than human in virtue both of their inferior ethnicity and their inferior sex or gender. Note Shrage's evasive use of the passives "seen as" and "regarded as," without attaching a "by" clause. By whom, exactly? Seen as less than human by society (whatever that means)? By the john himself? But his visiting a black prostitute might mean that he, Jesus-like, values that which society does not value. What makes Shrage suppose that anyone other than herself has internalized these crude traditional judgments? And if she hasn't internalized them, why does she think that others have or do, in particular the men who visit black prostitutes?

Shrage also claims that "in our own culture we define a woman's participation in sexual activity for a motive other than love as prostitution."[73] *We* do? This howler gives Shrage away: it shows that she has no grasp of social reality, which fact helps explain her fatuous propositions about interracial prostitution. Who is this "we" that embraces that definition, other than Shrage? Perhaps what Shrage meant is that "we" call or judge women who engage in sex for a motive other than love—for example, out of her own sexual desire— "sluts'" or "whores." But "we" don't do that; only some of us, sexual conservatives, do. Even so, to assert that such a woman is a "whore" is not to assert that she engages in "prostitution"; it is to assert only that she has *one* thing in common with prostitutes, that she engages in (promiscuous) sex without love. See the very first example presented by the etymologist Julie Coleman in her lexicographic monstrosity *Love, Sex, and Marriage*:

[F]or us a *prostitute* is a woman who is paid for having sex. The emphasis is on payment; so much so, that a woman who does not have sex with her clients, but merely dresses up for them, or dominates them, would still be called a prostitute. For *earlier* periods, the defining feature of prostitution has been having sex, not being paid for it, so a woman who was only promiscuous could be labelled a *whore*.[74]

Yes. But that was true a few generations ago, not true for the generation about which Shrage uses her reckless "we."

NOTES

1. Steve Martin, "Does God Exist?" *New Yorker* (December 7 & 14, 1998): 100.

2. Catharine A. MacKinnon, *Feminism Unmodified: Discourses on Life and Law* (Cambridge: Harvard University Press, 1987), p. 262; see also p. 176. More recently, see MacKinnon, "Pornography Left and Right," in *Sex, Preference, and Family: Essays on Law and Nature*, ed. David M. Estlund and Martha C. Nussbaum (New York: Oxford University Press, 1997), p. 120 n. 55.

3. Andrea Dworkin and Catharine A. MacKinnon, *Pornography and Civil Rights: A New Day for Women's Equality* (Minneapolis, Minn.: Organizing Against Pornography, 1988), p. 37.

4. Ibid., p. 39.

5. See Buchard of Worms, quoted in Pierre J. Payer, *The Bridling of Desire: Views of Sex in the Later Middle Ages* (Toronto: University of Toronto Press, 1993), p. 220 n. 74.

6. Andrea Dworkin, *Intercourse* (New York: Free Press, 1987), p. 138.

7. Susan M. Easton, *The Problem of Pornography: Regulation and the Right to Free Speech* (London: Routledge, 1994), pp. 116–17.

8. See Harriett Gilbert: "Dworkin's book [*Mercy*] is hard to distinguish from its predecessor [Sade's *Justine*]: a work which . . . many would suppose to fulfil every one of Dworkin's criteria for

pornography" ("So Long as It's Not Sex and Violence: Andrea Dworkin's *Mercy*," in *Sex Exposed: Sexuality and the Pornography Debate*, ed. Lynne Segal and Mary McIntosh [New Brunswick, N.J.: Rutgers University Press, 1993], p. 216).

9. See Roger Scruton, *Sexual Desire: A Moral Philosophy of the Erotic* (New York: Free Press, 1986): "the lurid dildos which are on display in sex shops . . . have precisely no *sexual* appeal to the person of normal inclinations" (p. 28).

10. It is not quite right to criticize one or two items on MacKinnon and Dworkin's list of sexual atrocities and to say that the writers went too far here, or there, and the list would have been better had these curious and apparently disposable items not been included. For the original inclusion of these items ("being penetrated by objects") is a sign of the type of thinking or attitude that informed the construction of the list, a sign of the guiding principle that ties all the items together. The odd item in the MacKinnon-Dworkin definition is the revealing item: it shows the sexually conservative rationale for the whole list.

11. Ann Garry, "Pornography and Respect for Women," in *Philosophy and Women*, ed. Sharon Bishop and Marjorie Weinzweig (Belmont, Calif.: Wadsworth, 1979), p. 137.

12. Susan Griffin, *Pornography and Silence: Culture's Revenge against Nature* (New York: Harper and Row, 1981), p. 38.

13. Ibid., p. 61.

14. See James Weaver: The "common theme" of "standard pornography" is "female-instigated sex" ("The Social Science and Psychological Research Evidence: Perceptual and Behavioural Consequences of Exposure to Pornography," in *Pornography: Women, Violence and Civil Liberties*, ed. Catherine Itzin [Oxford: Oxford University Press, 1992], p. 300).

15. See Robin Morgan: "I claim that rape exists any time sexual intercourse occurs when it has not been initiated by the woman, out of her own genuine affection and desire" ("Theory and Practice: Pornography and Rape," in *Going Too Far: The Personal Chronicle of a Feminist* [New York: Random House, 1977], p. 165; italics omitted).

16. Dworkin and MacKinnon, *Pornography and Civil Rights*, p. 46.

17. Nadine Strossen, *Defending Pornography: Free Speech, Sex, and the Fight for Women's Rights* (New York: Scribner, 1995), p. 162.

18. Linda Williams, *Hard Core: Power, Pleasure, and the "Frenzy of the Visible"* (Berkeley: University of California Press, 1989), p. 154.

19. Mary Jane Sherfey, *The Nature and Evolution of Female Sexuality* (New York: Vintage, 1973), pp. 108–14, 134–40.

20. See Ferrel M. Christensen, "Cultural and Ideological Bias in Pornography Research," *Philosophy of the Social Sciences* 20, no. 3 (1990): 357.

21. Dolf Zillmann and Jennings Bryant, "Effects of Massive Exposure to Pornography," in *Pornography and Sexual Aggression*, ed. Neil M. Malamuth and Edward Donnerstein (Orlando, Fla.: Academic Press, 1984), p. 135.

22. James Check, "The Effects of Violent Pornography, Nonviolent Dehumanizing Pornography, and Erotica: Some Legal Implications from a Canadian Perspective," in *Pornography: Women, Violence and Civil Liberties*, ed. Catherine Itzin (Oxford: Oxford University Press, 1992), pp. 350–51.

23. Scruton, *Sexual Desire*, p. 139.

24. Judith Searle, "Penis Envy," *Cosmopolitan* (June 1975): 189. See William Ian Miller, *The Anatomy of Disgust* (Cambridge: Harvard University Press, 1997), p. 128.

25. *Final Report of the Attorney General's Commission on Pornography* (Nashville, Tenn.: Rutledge Hill Press, 1986), p. 41.

26. Ibid., p. 41 n. 46.

27. Margaret Jean Intons-Peterson and Beverly Roskos-Ewoldsen also propose a tripartite division that leaves no conceptual room for depictions of selfish women: "[W]e classify pornography into . . . erotica, pornography, and violent pornography. . . . Erotica portrays nonaggressive sexual activity between willing, sensitive, caring partners. The partners share in the initiation and choice of activities, relatively free from the stereotypic pattern of male dominance and female subservience that characterizes much pornography." In pornography, "[w]omen are the slaves, the sexual playthings, for men to use and discard. . . . Their chief interest is the satisfaction of male sexual desire" ("Mitigating the

Effects of Violent Pornography," in *For Adult Users Only: The Dilemma of Violent Pornography*, ed. Susan Gubar and Joan Hoff [Bloomington: Indiana University Press, 1989], p. 219).

28. *Final Report*, p. 43.

29. Diana E. H. Russell, "Introduction," in *Making Violence Sexy: Feminist Views on Pornography*, ed. Diana E. H. Russell (New York: Teachers College Press, 1993), p. 3.

30. In his detective-murder novel *The Moving Toyshop* (New York: Penguin Books, 1958), Edmund Crispin imagines that his protagonist, Gervase Fen, Oxford Professor of English and Literature, proposes a game to the poet Richard Cadogan: "Detestable Characters in Fiction. Both players must agree, and each player has five seconds in which to think of a character. . . . They must be characters the author intended to be sympathetic" (p. 55). The first answer Fen provides is "Lady Chatterley and that gamekeeper fellow." Cadogan replies, "Yes" (p. 56).

31. Russell, "Introduction," p. 3. See also Charlene Y. Senn, "The Research on Women and Pornography: The Many Faces of Harm," in *Making Violence Sexy: Feminist Views on Pornography*, ed. Diana E. H. Russell (New York: Teachers College Press, 1993), p. 181: "*Nonviolent Pornography—Sexist and Dehumanizing*" includes images of "male fully dressed, female naked."

32. Russell, "Introduction," p. 3. The passage continues with other examples, but these are enough to make the point. See also Russell's "Pornography and Rape: A Causal Model," *Political Psychology* 9, no. 1 (1988): 56, in which she credits Edna Einsiedel with the facial ejaculation example.

33. Catherine Itzin, "Editor's Introduction" to "District Court of Ontario, *R. v. Ross Wise*, before the Hon. Judge H. R. Locke, 22 June 1990: Reasons for Judgment," in *Pornography: Women, Violence and Civil Liberties*, ed. Catherine Itzin (Oxford: Oxford University Press, 1992), p. 604. For these images, see alt.binaries.pictures.erotica.facials and alt.binaries.nospam.facials. Itzin would be especially repulsed by Japanese "bukkake" pornography, in which a group of men deposit their ejaculate on one woman's face.

34. Strossen, *Defending Pornography*, p. 154.

35. Miller, *Anatomy of Disgust*, p. 28; see also pp. 104–105.

36. See Edward O. Laumann et al., *The Social Organization of Sexuality: Sexual Practices in the United States* (Chicago: University of Chicago Press, 1994), Table 4.2, pp. 152–53, and Table 4.3, especially p. 163; and Robert T. Michael et al., *Sex in America* (Boston: Little, Brown and Company, 1994), p. 153: among women in the age group 18–44 years, less than one-fifth said they found giving oral sex to a man "very appealing."

37. Forty percent of those students studied at Indiana University do not think that oral sex is "having sex." See Stephanie Sanders and June Reinisch, "Would You Say You 'Had Sex' If . . . ?" *Journal of the American Medical Association* 281, no. 3 (January 20, 1999): 275–77. Perhaps they think this because, in fellatio to completion, the ejaculate is deposited elsewhere than inside a vagina.

38. Sigmund Freud, *Three Essays on the Theory of Sexuality*, in *The Standard Edition of the Complete Psychological Works of Sigmund Freud*, ed. and trans. James Strachey (London: Hogarth Press, 1953–74), vol. 7, p. 186.

39. Sigmund Freud, "On the Universal Tendency to Debasement in the Sphere of Love," in ibid., vol. 11, p. 189.

40. From William Butler Yeats, "Crazy Jane Talks with the Bishop," in *The Collected Poems of W. B. Yeats*, ed. Richard J. Finneran (New York: Macmillan, 1989), pp. 259–60.

41. Pat Califia, in her short story "Jessie," which is about a sexual encounter between two women, describes this scenario: While Liz is sitting on the toilet, peeing, Jessie's "arms tightened around me [Liz], and I knew the sound was arousing her. It was a very intimate moment. I felt closer to her then than I've felt to some women who had their tongues in my mouth. . . . [S]he wiped me neatly" (in *Macho Sluts* [Los Angeles: Alyson Books, 1988], p. 51).

42. Vincent C. Punzo, "Morality and Human Sexuality," in *Social Ethics: Morality and Social Policy*, 5th ed., ed. Thomas A. Mappes and Jane S. Zembaty (New York: McGraw-Hill, 1997), p. 158; see also p. 159. I assume that by heterosexual "sexual intercourse" Punzo means "coitus"—see his expression "entered her." If, which seems unlikely, Punzo means "sexual intercourse" in a

broad sense, as including any type of sexual activity between a male and a female, not just coitus, then just engaging in sexual activity of any form is, for him, the most intimate thing two people, a male and a female, can do with each other. Janice Moulton seems to have something similar in mind: "Sexual behavior differs from other behavior by virtue of its unique feelings and emotions and its unique ability to create shared intimacy" ("Sexual Behavior: Another Position," in *The Philosophy of Sex: Contemporary Readings*, 3rd ed., ed. Alan Soble [Lanham, Md.: Rowman and Littlefield, 1997], p. 37).

It follows from such a view that one would be hard-pressed to grade the various possible heterosexual sexual acts in terms of the physical intimacy each involves. It would also follow, contrary to Punzo's restricting intimate sexual acts to those done between a man and woman, that homosexuals, too, could experience the sublime intimacy that sexual activity allows or promotes. Punzo thus has a sexual-political reason for insisting that he means "sexual intercourse" in its narrow sense.

Given the conservative implications (if not purpose) of Punzo's argument, it is noteworthy that the feminist philosopher Louise Collins draws on his essay in defending her own views that "sex offers an unique context for re-integrating one's physical and psychological person" and that "sex should be cherished as a special medium for expressing love" ("Emotional Adultery: Cybersex and Commitment," *Social Theory and Practice* 25, no. 2 [1999]: 249; see p. 266 n. 21). This type of agreement between the conservative Punzo and the self-categorized feminist Collins is no longer surprising. In chapter 4 I discuss the reliance of feminist objections to pornography on the hoary sex-love connection.

43. Gilbert Meilaender, *The Limits of Love: Some Theological Explorations* (University Park: Pennsylvania State University Press, 1987), p. 47.

44. Some interesting ink has been spilled about gay male fistfucking. Richard Mohr, for example, sees the anal fisting portrayed in Robert Mapplethorpe's photograph *Helmut and Brooks* as a marriage portrait (*Gay Ideas* [Boston: Beacon Press, 1992], p. 188). And

while explicating the thought of Michael Foucault, David Halperin speaks of anal fisting as a sort of "anal yoga" and as a sexual act that "decentralizes" and de-phallocizes male bodily pleasure (*Saint Foucault: Towards a Gay Hagiography* [New York: Oxford University Press, 1995], pp. 90–91).

45. "A person's tongue in your mouth could be experienced as a pleasure or as a most repulsive and nauseating intrusion depending on the state of relations that exist or are being negotiated between you and the [other] person. But someone else's tongue in your mouth can be a sign of intimacy, *because* it can also be a disgusting assault" (Miller, *Anatomy of Disgust*, p. 137).

46. Scruton, *Sexual Desire*, p. 151.

47. Nicholas Lemann, "Southern Discomfort," *New Yorker* (March 13, 2000): 95.

48. See Dan Sabbath and Mandel Hall, *End Product: The First Taboo* (New York: Urizen Books, 1977), pp. 157–59. The contemporary analytic philosopher Robert Nozick is refreshingly candid:

> [P]rofound emotions are awakened and expressed in sex. The trust involved in showing our own pleasures, the vulnerability in letting another give us these and guide them, including pleasures with infantile or oedipal reverberations, or anal ones, does not come lightly.

"Sexuality," in *The Examined Life* (New York: Simon and Schuster, 1989), p. 62.

49. D. H. Lawrence, *Lady Chatterley's Lover* (New York: New American Library, 1962), pp. 208–209. See the passage also in Martha C. Nussbaum, "Objectification," in *The Philosophy of Sex: Contemporary Readings*, 3rd ed., ed. Alan Soble (Lanham, Md.: Rowman and Littlefield, 1997), p. 314. This passage from *Lady Chatterley's Lover* was strangely omitted from the version of this essay that Nussbaum reprinted in her *Sex and Social Justice* (New York: Oxford University Press, 1999), p. 239.

50. See Lawrence, *Lady Chatterley's Lover*, pp. 66, 208–209, 218–19, 248, 259.

51. Itzin, "Editor's Introduction," p. 604.

52. See Scott O'Hara: "for gay men, all through history, having

our mouths full of dick has been a political statement like no other. . . . Sucking dick is still the perfect expression of our First Amendment rights" ("Talking with My Mouth Full," in *Policing Public Sex: Queer Politics and the Future of AIDS Activism*, ed. Ephen Glenn Colter et al. [Boston: South End Press, 1996], p. 81).

53. Catharine A. MacKinnon, "Feminism, Marxism, Method, and the State: An Agenda for Theory," in *Feminist Theory: A Critique of Ideology*, ed. Nannerl O. Keohane, Michelle Z. Rosaldo, and Barbara C. Gelpi (Chicago: University of Chicago Press, 1982), p. 18. MacKinnon's claim, as does Itzin's, requires a bloated notion of coercion; see my *Sexual Investigations* (New York: New York University Press, 1986), pp. 244–47.

54. According to Lillian Rubin, most women who try anal intercourse (only 30 percent of women even try it) find it too painful, yet some women perceive it as providing a "special thrill" (*Erotic Wars: What Happened to the Sexual Revolution?* [New York: Farrar, Straus and Giroux, 1990], p. 125).

55. Morgan, "Theory and Practice," pp. 167–68. Gayle Rubin remarks, in a plea for tolerance in matters sexual, that "people who are not into anal sex find it incomprehensible that anyone else could enjoy it" ("The Leather Menace: Comments on Politics and S/M," in *Coming to Power*, ed. Samois [Palo Alto, Calif.: Up Press, 1981], p. 221).

56. Nussbaum, "Objectification," pp. 303, 318 n. 42.

57. Park Elliott Dietz, "Statement of Park Elliott Dietz," in *Final Report of the Attorney General's Commission on Pornography* (Nashville, Tenn.: Rutledge Hill Press, 1986), p. 489.

58. Ibid.

59. Ibid., pp. 491–92.

60. Some of Shere Hite's respondents speak favorably of anilingis, others unfavorably; see her *The Hite Report on Male Sexuality* (New York: Alfred A. Knopf, 1981), pp. 592–93. In the huge study of sexual behavior carried out at the University of Chicago, anilingis was not even investigated; subjects were asked only about anal intercourse and anal fingering. I suppose it was too gross to mention in a sophisticated sociological survey. See Laumann et al., *Social Organization of Sexuality*, p. 158.

61. Erica Jong, *Fear of Flying* (New York: Signet, 1973).

62. Dolf Zillmann and Jennings Bryant observe that "the principle message of pornography [is that] great sexual joy and ecstasy are accessible to parties who just met, who are in no way committed to each other, and who will part shortly, never to meet again" ("Pornography's Impact on Sexual Satisfaction," *Journal of Applied Social Psychology* 18, no. 5 [1988]: 450).

63. Dietz, "Statement of Park Elliott Dietz," p. 489.

64. See Linda Williams: "[T]he not-so-hidden agenda of the Meese Commission report is to condemn those unorthodox sexualities that can be construed as perverse. Commissioner Park Elliott Dietz states his abhorrence of such unorthodoxy clearly" (*Hard Core*, p. 19). Williams continues, " 'Normal' sexuality, the commission implies, is never violent, not even in the imagination," in which passage she recognizes the *eros* of the sexual.

65. Jeanne Barkey and J. Koplin," 'Entertainment' for Men: What It Is and What It Means," in *Pornography: Women, Violence and Civil Liberties*, ed. Catherine Itzin (Oxford: Oxford University Press, 1992), p. 38. The authors of this essay are given only in the "Copyright Credits," p. 636.

66. See Linda Williams, "Sexual Politics: Strange Bedfellows," *In These Times* (October 29–November 4, 1986): 18–20, for some analysis of the convergence of antipornography feminism and conservatism.

67. Laurie Shrage, "Is Sexual Desire Raced?: The Social Meaning of Interracial Prostitution," *Journal of Social Philosophy* 23, no. 1 (1992): 44, 45.

68. Geoffrey Chaucer, "The Wife of Bath's Prologue," in *The Canterbury Tales*, trans. Nevill Coghill (Baltimore: Penguin Books, 1961), p. 288.

69. There is nothing about interracial prostitution in Laumann et al., *Social Organization of Sexuality* (see pp. 262–64 on the frequency of interracial sexual relations) or in Hite, *Hite Report on Male Sexuality* (see pp. 759–76 on prostitution).

70. Daphne Merkin, "Sister Act," *New Yorker* (June 14, 1999): 84. In her review of my *Sexual Investigations*, Cheshire Calhoun

protests: "[Soble] appears to think that the way to find out what pornography means is to ask individual men what they are explicitly thinking when they view pornography. This is an oddly solipsistic view of meaning" (*Ethics* 109, no. 4 [1999]: 930). No. Imagining or guessing what men are thinking when they view pornography, instead of asking them, is the solipsistic domination by some of the ignored minds of others.

71. Shrage, "Is Sexual Desire Raced?" p. 46. For more feminist political analysis of prostitution, see Carole Pateman, *The Sexual Contract* (Stanford, Calif.: Stanford University Press, 1988), p. 199, and my critique in *Sexual Investigations*, p. 87.

72. Shrage, "Is Sexual Desire Raced?" p. 48.

73. Ibid., p. 49.

74. Julie Coleman, *Love, Sex, and Marriage: A Historical Thesaurus* (Amsterdam: Rodopi, 1999), p. i (italics added for "earlier").

FOUR

CHESLER'S COMPLAINT, FANTASY, <u>PLAYBOY</u>

Women are insatiable. We are greedy. Our appetites do need to be controlled if things are to stay in place. If the world were ours too, if we believed we could get away with it, we would ask for more love, more sex, more money.

Naomi Wolf[1]

FUDGING

The sociologist Diana E. H. Russell has, as a feminist antipornography activist, written a great deal about the sexually degrading content of pornographic images, some of whose claims we have examined. She has also condemned the production and consumption of pornography on the basis of the harmful effects of sexual material. For example, at one point in an essay that criticizes pornography, Russell writes:

Another tribute to the mainstreaming of pornography in contemporary U. S. is [Lillian B.] Rubin's finding that about 25% of her sample "said they had experimented with some form of bondage," particularly those under 35 years of age (1990, p. 128).[2]

What is the causal order between the occurrence of bondage images in pornography and the incidence of bondage in people's sexual lives? Russell surely does not know that people engage in bondage sexuality exactly because they see such things depicted in pornography, although her antipornography feminism requires that causal connection to be true and she implies that pornography causes people to engage in these nasty sexual behaviors. At any rate, Russell does not give us the richness of the sociologist Rubin's account, but fudges in merely reporting a bare fact in a manner that gains advantage in making a case against pornography. Here is the relevant passage in Rubin:

> About a quarter of the study's population said they had experimented with some form of bondage, an activity more prominent in the under-35 groups than in the older one. Sometimes it was nothing more than one partner or the other being pinned down with hands over the head. . . . Sometimes people tied each other up, both men and women saying they enjoyed the dominance and submission side of the game equally well. "I can enjoy being tied up, and I like tying someone up," said 25-year-old Felicia, a New York editorial assistant. "It's part of the whole fantasy—sometimes to be the dominant one and then to turn it around into submission."[3]

From Rubin's original, we get quite a different picture than we do from Russell's brief and misleading reproduction of a fact. Rubin's account allows us to appreciate that the interest in bondage and power is gender-neutral, that an interest in dominating a sexual partner is not restricted to men. Another woman in Rubin's study, a twenty-three-year-old typist in Los Angeles, dislikes being bound for sex. "But I love to tie someone else up and have him in my power," she reveals.[4] Further, Rubin's subjects appear to conceive of and treat bondage sexuality as a *game*, as a lighthearted supplement to their more ordinary sexual activities. There does not seem much to be concerned about here, and surely Rubin's fact provides no evidence for a troublesome "mainstreaming of pornography."

Russell did not do a good job of relaying to her readers information provided by another sociologist, one of her colleagues; information that might be of some importance. I have found this often in the literature, that antipornography feminists twist the empirical research to their own benefit.[5] Yet, perhaps predictably in the context of such a heated debate, feminist antipornographers level the same accusation against those that defend pornography. For example, consider the accusations made by Catherine Itzin and the philosopher Cynthia Stark:

> Attempts to distort and misrepresent the evidence that exists of the harm caused by pornography range from denying that it exists to claiming that it does but that it is inconclusive. . . . Denying or discrediting the evidence of harm is an essential strategy of pro-pornography interests because it is on the basis of this evidence that action is most likely to be taken against pornography.[6]

> It is hard to resist the conclusion that those who remain skeptical about the empirical evidence [linking pornography to behaviors and attitudes harmful to women] are motivated by nothing more than the desire to have pornography available.[7]

In reply to Itzin, it would be fair to mention that she omits one category of distortion, the distortion carried out by antipornography feminists who exaggerate the type and extent of the harm caused by pornography (for example, Russell's distortion of Rubin). Intellectual honesty would have us admit this type of distortion as well, if the other two types exist. And in reply to Stark, one might plausibly claim that the reason for not taking the harm research more seriously is, in part, that both feminists and conservatives have manipulated the data in advancing their social and political agendas. It is grossly uncharitable for Stark to imply that defenders of pornography who are "skeptical" of the harm research are unbelieving precisely because these perverts do not want to lose access to their favorite source of sexual pleasure. Permit me to provide some other, decent reasons for remaining skeptical.

Russell has done her own sociological research on the harmful effects of pornography. In attempting to study the effects of men's consumption of pornography on heterosexual relationships, Russell asked this question of 929 women in the San Francisco area: "Have you ever been upset by anyone trying to get you to do what they'd seen in pornographic pictures, movies, or books?" Ten percent of Russell's women subjects answered "yes."[8] Russell and those who have employed her research in their antipornography campaigns implicitly emphasize that a *full* 10 percent of the women answered "yes" to this question.[9] But, of course, it is just as, if not more, plausible to emphasize, with either relief or regret, that *only* 10 percent of the women answered "yes," they had been upset. Russell's numbers, at least, are not very impressive, and if it was a mere ten percent in big city, pornography-infused San Francisco, how much less frequently would a "yes" have been heard in, for example, Bogalusa, Louisiana, or McComb, Mississippi?

There are a number of other problems in Russell's research that deserve examination. One set of problems arises about the sort of "trying" on the part of men that Russell had in mind when asking her question or, more significantly, what sort of "trying" her women subjects remembered or imagined. The feminist scholar and author Pauline

Bart thinks she knows what "trying" means. In her testimony supporting the antipornography Ordinance drafted by Catharine MacKinnon and Andrea Dworkin, Bart claimed that she was in favor of the Ordinance in part

> because Diana Russell found that 10 percent of the women in her sample . . . had been asked to do, or demanded to do, something they did not want to do because the person asking them had read about it in pornography.[10]

Several fudges ruin this testimony. There is a big difference, to start, between a man's asking a woman to engage in a certain sexual activity and his demanding that she do so (both are types of "trying"). If the problem uncovered by Russell is that men *demand* of women what they see in pornographic images, then the objection is not necessarily to the nature of the sexual activity that the men would like to do but to the manner in which the men attempt to get the women to accommodate these desires. That pornography contains images of sexual acts that women do not find appealing, then, seems irrelevant. The women may not have been upset at the proposed sexual activity itself; instead, they might have been upset at their being demanded to do it. In this case, pornography is not the issue, but the crudity of men—unless, which is not obviously true, consuming pornography causes men to cross the line from asking for something from women to demanding it from them. Note also that if some of the 10 percent of the women who were upset were merely asked to do things, and others were demanded to do them, on Bart's dichotomous interpretation of Russell, we would like to know what portion of the 10 percent fell into each category. For if the problem is that men demand that women perform sexually for them, the percent of women who have experienced this pressure must be less than 10 percent, making the problem even less statistically interesting. One more fudge: the question Russell asked of her women subjects referred to their being "upset," yet Bart changes this to their being asked or demanded to do something they did not *want* to do. Of course, if a woman does not want to do a certain sexual act, she might very well be upset if her lover or husband wants to do it and makes that desire or intention plain to her. But being upset at a proposal to do something sexual and not wanting or liking to do it are not the same thing. Specifically, if the women were upset exactly because the men demanded that they perform sexually for them, whether the women liked or wanted to do the act demanded of them is beside the point. A woman might enjoy fellatio and ordinarily or otherwise want to do it, yet feel upset if her partner demands that she do it. Bart's testimony in favor of antipornography legislation is not faithful to the study that she cites, and falls short of what we expect from members of the academy.

A second set of problems revolves around what the women actually knew when they answered "yes," that their men had asked for, or demanded, "what they'd seen in" pornography. How does any woman actually come to know that what her partner has proposed was introduced to his mind or added to his desires by his consuming pornography? And how do we know that she knows? When the social psychologists Dolf Zillmann and Jennings Bryant write about Russell's research that "men were *found* to have made women comply with their requests to try what they had seen" in pornography,[11] they overlook that Russell could have recorded only women's *beliefs* that their men were inspired by what they had seen in pornography. These beliefs could have anything from decent to poor epistemic warrant. For example, if a man and a woman are together watching a pornographic video in which a woman performs anilingis on a man, and the viewing man immediately suggests to his female partner that she do it to him, right then and there, she has good reason to think that his watching that particular video at that particular moment induced him (but did not determine him) to express a desire for the act. But if she has discovered a handful of pornographic magazines in his bottom desk drawer, that discovery by itself should give her little reason to think that any of his sexual requests were induced by his consuming pornography—although she might believe it anyway, and report that belief in a Russell-style survey. Further, in relation to both cases, the man's interest in pornography and his requesting sexual activities from her might both be the result of his prepornographic sexual desires, desires whose possible origins are legion. Indeed, since the idea behind a man's request for a particular sexual performance from a woman might have come from myriad sources—mainstream television programs, Hollywood movies or those shown on PBS or the A&E channel, *Lady Chatterley's Lover*, the Old Testament, his mother or father or cousin or other lovers, maybe those in his past—it becomes unclear whether the problem that Russell has uncovered is that women are upset exactly because the sexual proposals they get from their men come from pornography, or that women are upset at their men's requests regardless where the men get their sexual ideas and desires. Is it less upsetting for a woman if her partner's sexual proposals are historically tied with what he did at the request of a previous lover than if he were introduced to it by viewing it on a pornographic Internet site? I am not convinced that a man's expecting or hoping for more and varied sexual activities from his female partner is an objectionable consequence of his consumption of pornography, if (which is largely true) it is not an unobjectionable consequence of many other events and experiences in his biography that round out his sexual nature (for example, that he heard about some acts from a more experienced friend or lover, or from a psychology or medical textbook).

Russell's loaded question to her women subjects, then, obscures more than it clarifies sexual problems in heterosexual relationships. Is the problem that consuming pornography induces men to propose that women engage in deviant, disgusting, and perverted sexual activities, and the women find such acts upsetting to contemplate? My guess is that men would have expressed and do express these decadent desires anyway. Is the problem primarily that women are upset when they are pressured into performing sexually, so that if their men want to try something perverse, the least they could do is to ask nicely? Or is the problem not in the kind of "trying" that is used or in the nature of the sexual activity proposed, but rather exactly in its origin in pornographic images? Given the confusion in Russell's question and the resulting uncertainty about what a "yes" answer means, one would expect her to be cautious. But what we get is an astounding conclusion. According to Russell, the women who answered the question in the affirmative "felt that they had been personally victimized by pornography,"[12] and Russell implies that for her this (purported) effect of pornography is reprehensible and intolerable. But even if we grant that the consumption of pornography was involved in making these women upset, that does not justify such a judgment.

Three conceptual or philosophical distinctions that are crucial here—which Russell ignores—are those between (1) *legitimate* and *illegitimate* feelings of being upset, (2) *beneficial* and *harmful* feelings of being upset, and, most crucially, (3) merely *feeling* victimized and actually *being* victimized. Sometimes an upsetting experience is one that a person had a right not to undergo (perhaps finding one's spouse in bed with another person), and so his or her being upset seems to be a legitimate response; but at other times a person does not have such a right not to undergo an upsetting experience, and in these cases we might speak of the upset as an illegitimate response (perhaps finding a Goya nude on a Spanish adhesive in the spouse's stamp collection). Again, sometimes an upsetting experience is psychologically harmful, an unpleasant experience we would have been better off without (perhaps being exposed, with no advance warning, to one of the more dreadful, death-encrusted photographs of Joel-Peter Witkin); at other times an upsetting experience is productive, since it causes us to make a momentous decision or to change our lives, and is thereby an unpleasant experience that overall proves to be beneficial (perhaps finding our spouse in bed with his or her lover). Finally, merely *feeling* victimized is neither necessary nor sufficient for actually *being* victimized: accidentally overhearing an offensive, sexist remark coming from a person sitting in the next booth at a restaurant might make a woman feel victimized—especially if she is conversant in feminist theory—but that brief comment surely didn't make the woman a victim; and a woman might very well be a victim even if she has no feelings about or knowledge of her victimization, as when her husband sexually cheats on her cleverly and successfully avoids detection.

In order to criticize pornography for the kinds of effects found by Russell, one must argue—otherwise the assertions amount to not much more than whining—that the women's feelings of upset in response to their men's proposals were legitimate or harmful or in fact victimized them. And I do not see much future in that argument, unless we presuppose a sexually conservative position on the role of pornography in our lives and relationships. Indeed, a feminist, on pain of contradiction, cannot readily criticize pornographic literature, photographs, or films exactly on the grounds that they cause, either directly or indirectly, psychologically upsetting feelings. One common initial response of women who have been raised in traditional ways to feminist literature and thought is feeling upset and angry. Whether they have been imposed on, or their being upset is harmful or makes them victims, will depend on many other features of their situations. Occasionally the dissatisfaction with their lives provoked by feminist literature—some of which bluntly discusses sexual matters; some of which is sexually arousing—later results in divorce, or in a fresh career, or in a new, sometimes "woman-identified" or lesbian, lifestyle. Feminist philosophers, then, *need* the distinction between harmful and beneficial feelings of being upset and cannot use "upset" alone to criticize pornography or to claim that women are in this sense victimized by it. That a woman experiences discomfort and unpleasantness in response to a man's indelicate or clumsy sexual proposal does not mean that she has been a victim of wrongful discrimination or sexual harassment; merely being upset does not entail that one has been harassed, even if being harassed usually causes one to feel upset. The right not to be made uncomfortable by the actions and attitudes of others simply does not exist, in either law or morality, and should not be conflated with a right not to be sexually harassed.[13]

A more recent psychological investigation carried out by Charlene Senn commits similar errors. Senn showed different kinds of pornography to a whopping ninety-six undergraduate women subjects. She reports:

> Mood disturbance scores were compared across the four groups of women (erotica, nonviolent pornography, violent pornography, and control). . . . [N]o difference was found between the pornography groups on the amount of emotional disturbance caused. Exposure to both violent pornography *and* nonviolent pornography was found to cause significant mood disturbance in women. . . . [They] were found to make women more tense and anxious, more

angry and hostile, and more confused. Viewing violent pornography also increased women's level of depression.[14]

These findings, if reliable, are noteworthy, although we should be careful in what we do with or infer from them. One step that Senn takes, which might to some seem innocent and reasonable enough, is questionable: She automatically promotes the anger, hostility, tension, and anxiety induced in women by their viewing pornography to the level of harm: "The emotional affects of pornography may be even more harmful than they appear on the surface." But, we know quite well, many things have the emotional affect of anger and anxiety and so forth without thereby being harmful either immediately or in the long run: For one example, a lecture in an introductory philosophy class, let alone a lecture in a philosophy of feminism or sexuality class. Yet Senn elaborates the meaning of her laboratory study in the most dramatic way possible, hinting that censorship of pornography is warranted in light of the terrible harms women suffer when they view it:

> Women are harmed directly when they view pornography. . . . [W]hen women view these materials the result is emotional distress. . . . These harms are specific to sexual materials that include sexism and/or violence. . . . My hope is that the research being done on women for women on pornography will . . . help us to prove to the world that the harms done to women by pornography are harms so great that no society could defend them.[15]

My hope is that Senn does not mean her implicit major premise seriously, that anything that causes these types of emotional states (which she calls "harms") is indefensible. These psychological effects might be specific to sexist and violent sexual materials *among sexual materials*, but they are surely not specific to sexual materials. Men might experience these effects, too, even as they masturbate with pleasure to pornographic images. Women might not experience this emotional distress at all, were they to look more often at pornography. I wonder if the writer Sallie Tisdale and the film critic Linda Williams found that their reactions to pornography evolved as they looked more closely and comprehensively at sexual images, not in the psychologist's laboratory at the university but in the familiar surroundings of their homes. Were Senn's distressed subjects merely pornographically or sexually uninitiated? In any event, women can avoid the purported harmful distress caused by pornography not only by looking at pornography more often but also by not looking at pornography at all. No one must eat asparagus if he or she dislikes it, and of course it would be wrong, ceteris paribus, to force those stalks down someone's throat—or to cajole female subjects to participate in a study of the harmful effects of looking at pornography.

Being, or being made, anxious, hostile, tense, and angry per se does not count as harm or being harmed. Sometimes, to repeat the obvious, emotional distress is in the long haul good for us. Whether emotional distress counts as harm, or whether it is a kind of harm we should worry about and eradicate, is context sensitive: why and how the emotional distress is brought about or arises, what the distress in turn leads to, how much distress is produced, and so forth. Senn must agree that whether this harm is something to be avoided altogether, and is indefensible, is context sensitive, because on her own account she, as the investigator, caused harmful emotional distress to her subjects by showing them pornography. Senn might reply that her subjects volunteered; but the reliance on consent breaks the connection between emotional distress and harm, or eliminates the moral punch of the harm. Senn would be rejecting her major premise (that anything that causes unpleasant mental states is wrong). Or Senn might reply that she had a good purpose in mind while harming her subjects; but, if so, the preeminence of these goals also breaks the connection between distress and harm, or eliminates the moral punch of harm. Again she would be rejecting her major premise. Or Senn, finally, might resort to disingenuousness: She might reply that before her study she had absolutely no idea or suspicion that pornography would cause emotional distress to her subjects, that she was completely taken by surprise.

THE LIFE OF RILEY

The feminist author Phyllis Chesler has uncovered what she takes to be a harmful effect of pornography. In the relations between the sexes, there is, according to the sociologist Rubin, a psychological disparity: Men are emotionally reserved or withdrawn and fear intimacy, while women are emotionally expressive and crave intimacy.[16] Chesler fastens on the male side when complaining about the sexuality of middle-aged men:

> There are no older women in pornography.[17] The largest female complaint in the liberal sector about men is not that men are brutal, violent, sadistic. . . . The big female complaint is that men at home in bed are emotionally passive. They are not there. They are somewhere else. They are distant. They are imagining someone else, someone much younger with no hair, someone with no flaws, not an adult female. Men are not with us. I do not know for sure whether this leads to pornography or pornography leads to this. I do know that it leads to the enormous psychological suffering of women.[18]

Chesler does not say here whether men sexually withdraw from older women because of the allure of pornography, or men turn to pornography because of their lack of sexual interest in older women, or pornography has made them critical of and less sexually arousable by older women.[19] Maybe all are true. Chesler does write elsewhere, however, that pornography "hampers men's abilities to relate in intimate and nourishing ways, particularly when they marry."[20] In any event, women experience "enormous" psychological suffering by men's sexual withdrawal, but to say that women are psychologically damaged by men's sexuality is suspiciously envious of the sexual attractiveness of younger women and resentful of the men who have or want them. Chesler's Complaint is not that men are physically cruel; instead, they are sexually disinterested, that is, psychologically cruel. Women are still the victims of male sexuality—or the *lack* of it.[21] Yet women, too, in the midst of sexual intercourse or oral sex with their men, often have private fantasies during which they become "distant" from their male partners. Where are they, exactly, when they drift away during orgasm—with Richard Gere or Denzell Washington on a wave-splashed beach instead of with their paunchy, balding male lovers? I do not suppose that these abandoned men also experience enormous psychological suffering; or, if they do, it's no big deal.

For Chesler, the suffering that results from psychologically and sexually absent husbands or partners unfairly or inequitably harms women:

A male version of menopause . . . , Don Juanism, . . . is an attempt to . . . flee from heterosexual intimacy.[22]

[M]en are impotent with grown women sexually, over a long period of time. They flee from intimacy with anyone who becomes a mother with whom they live under the same roof. And I am punished sexually by their withdrawal. They are not punished because they can run out to be turned on in strange, dark places by strange young women.[23]

Might Chesler believe that equality in "punishment" is the solution? If older women cannot have their older men, older men should not have access to young women, an alternative to their older women. Let's make the enormous psychological suffering equal even if more widespread, by eliminating the possibility that older men have younger women, in or out of pornography. But perhaps we can eliminate the suffering altogether (another form of equality) by encouraging women not to be so possessive and greedy (see epigraph). Instead of changing men, we could change women. Or we could try training men, in a process of reeroticization, to be turned on to near- and postmenopausal women, or provide older women with their own cadre of young, chivalrous men— strangers, prostitutes, with whom they can copulate on dark, deserted beaches. We might even make Chesler-pornography for older women, pornography that, fairy-tale style, depicts older women and their sexually attentive, same-age husbands. Without Cheslerian pornography, the genre will continue to cater to the sexual fantasies of those who consume it, men, and it will continue to declare that what our culture standardly promotes about marriage is an illusion or delusion, that the close intimacy and sexual pleasure in marriage desired by Chesler is not likely to be had. Dolf Zillmann and Jennings Bryant offer this bit of cautious wisdom:

Whether the creation [by pornography] of seemingly cynical beliefs and attitudes undermines social relationships by instilling distrust or, in fact, corrects erroneous, romantic, and idealistic views of human sexuality . . . cannot be decided one way or another by the data at hand.[24]

Their warning is, at least, more optimistic than Meese Commission member Park Dietz's opinion that nearly all pornography is dangerously false about human sexuality.

Why, exactly, are older men not much interested in sex with their older female partners? They fear and "flee from intimacy," is Chesler's pop-psychological answer. But the death of desire for the same, always available and often repeated, stimulus (sexual excitatory habituation) seems a more plausible explanation. The social psychologist Dolf Zillmann thankfully reports the obvious: "After years of monogamy . . . it is not uncommon for men to develop acute sexual disinterest—even secondary impotence."[25] He later adds, "It may seem ironic, but the characteristics of extended monogamous relationships that tend to be valued most highly (viz., being cared for, protected, and secure) are also those likely to foster drabness in sexual interaction."[26] The philosopher Roger Scruton goes radically farther: "People who have lived together in domestic intimacy feel a particular revulsion at the thought of contact between them."[27] Egads. Both men and women in long-term relationships can experience excitatory habituation, but in Chesler's world it is only women who are punished, the men running off to alleys to copulate with strange, disease-infested women. Humans have long grappled with the problem of the death of desire, some men and women (alone or together) attempting to solve the problem by seeking new partners or combinations of partners, by trying new sexual activities, or by exploring the universe of pornography.[28] Others die before excitatory habituation sets in, or they become accountants or programmers. Zillmann, one savvy psychologist, points out that "Acute pain . . . always can be counted on to stir up excitement. It is the habituation fighter par excellence. However, its exploitation demands limited usage."[29] Now that's a cute idea, a couple's saving their marriage by expanding their sexual repertoire into sadomasochism, not for any brutality per se but to instigate arousal by pushing the sexual body to its limits. Maybe older men would remain sexually faithful and sexually attentive if their older wives or partners agreed to play sadomasochist games in the bedroom. For Chesler, that would be to decrease the psychological brutality of sexual and emotional absenteeism by resorting to physical brutality (bondage? a spanking? you had worse as a kid, both at home and in the schoolyard, by those out of control, not in control, of themselves), which is hardly the cuddly copulatory intimacy she has in mind for pentogenarians. Women, forever victims, cannot win or even draw.

Some men (and women), even when they do not experience full-blown excitatory habituation toward their spouses or partners, still seek other sexual relationships or experiences, which fact must annoy anyone for whom devoted monogamy is ideal or obligatory. The art historian Camille Paglia observes that

> [g]ay men [in their promiscuity] are guardians of the masculine impulse. To have anonymous sex in a dark alleyway is to pay homage to the dream of male sexual freedom. . . . Similarly, straights who visit prostitutes are valiantly striving to keep sex free from emotion, duty, family—in other words, from society, religion, and procreative Mother Nature.[30]

Much the same can be said about men's interest in pornography, in two ways: it allows them to have sexual experiences that they strive to keep free of emotion, duty, family, society, religion, and procreative Mother Nature; and it allows them to have fantasies about women who are also liberated from emotion, duty, family, society, religion, and procreative Mother Nature.

In some respects, the use of pornography in masturbatory

sexuality more successfully than prostitution allows men to avoid emotion, duty, family, society, religion, and procreative Mother Nature. For in having sex with prostitutes, men can merely "strive" (Paglia's word) to be free of these things, but reality intrudes. Both the politically conservative (even antifeminist) Roger Scruton and the radical feminist Andrea Dworkin provide an unrealistic view of the relations between prostitute and client:

> Fantasies are private property, which I can dispose according to my will, with no answerability to the other whom I abuse through them. . . . For the fantasist, the ideal partner is indeed the prostitute, who, because she can be purchased, solves at once the moral problem presented by the presence of another at the scene of sexual release.[31]

> Prostitution: what is it? It is the use of a woman's body for sex by a man, he pays money, he does what he wants.[32]

But the prostitute is too often *not* compliant, not disposable "according to [the] will" of the client; nor does the client consistently get to "do what he wants."[33] The prostitute, many men discover, turns out to be a surface-slutty version of a bitchy, sexually stingy, and uptight wife, a repository of society's antisexualism, and is altogether selfishly interested in maximizing how much she can milk from the john without doing much milking herself. No wonder used and abused johns put them down by calling them "whores." It is an ignorant, romantic myth that whores are compliant, that men get whatever they want sexually from them. Street-smart prostitutes manipulate men and their desires, as if they were babes, using the psychological tricks of the trade; success for them is a piece of cake.[34] In pornography, by contrast, women are portrayed as not having to be talked or bribed or cajoled or lied to or begged (or forced) into having sex. Men avoid in pornographic sex the hassles of heterosexuality in a society that encourages women to be sly, deceptive, or otherwise less than candid before engaging in sex (sometimes in order to save face, sometimes in asserting their will to dominance). In the pornographic male fantasy of women's sexuality, men have sex, the kind of sex they want, with women who want sex for its own sake as much as they do and are not out to milk them financially.

This understanding of pornography, the truth in Margaret Baldwin's diatribe (see the beginning of chapter 1), has been expressed insightfully by media critic Laura Kipnis:

> [P]orno bimbos want to have sex all the time, with any guy no matter how disgusting, will do *anything*, moan like they like it, and aren't repulsed by male body fluids—in fact, adore them—wherever they land. Women who dislike pornography refer to this as a male fantasy, but what exactly is it a fantasy about? Well, it seems like a fantasy of a one-gender world, a world in which male and female sexuality is completely commensurable, as opposed to whatever sexual incompatibilities actually exist.[35]

Pornography, more than prostitution, offers men the headache-, PMS-, AIDS-less woman, sex without strings. The pornographic woman does not give men that look (or non-look) of sexual disdain and disgust that women use to put men down, to tell them, not very gently, and without any interest in allowing them to preserve a smidgen of the self-respect that they don't deserve anyway, that further interaction of any sort is absolutely out of the question—contrary to MacKinnon's view of the powerlessness of women to refuse men's overtures.[36] Pornography is popular not because it satisfies a desire that men purportedly have to dominate women, but because it allows them, in fantasy, to have all the good sex with them they want without the dangers, complications, and rejections. "[P]ornography offers an escape from the realities of sex itself."[37] The male fantasy of the accessible, horny, and perverse woman might be infantile, but so is bedroom sex, *eros* itself. Women, too, observes Naomi Wolf (in the epigraph), are greedy in bed. As does D. H. Lawrence: "They talk about a man's selfishness, but I doubt if it can ever touch a woman's blind beakishness, once she's gone that way."[38]

Men's flight from older women is roundly condemned by Chesler, as if it violated a universal moral law. From a woman's subjective perspective, male flight *is* condemnable, as contrary to her self-interest. No woman desires to "suffer" enormously from or be "punished" by a man's withdrawal, be it sexual, economic, or emotional. But it does not follow that the condemnation is warranted; not desiring to be emotionally and physically abandoned does not entail deserving not to be. A woman's interests and a man's interests are often in conflict and require balancing, which is not always possible.[39] Still, Chesler's Complaint, which asserts a link between men's interest in pornography and their fear of and flight from intimacy with adult women, has been milked by feminists for all it is worth. For Sara Diamond,

> pornography concentrates on fragments of the female form: a breast, foot, mouth. This allows the viewer to distance himself from the real person to whom the fragment belongs, avoiding the demands of relating to whole, intelligent, emotional and active women.[40]

Well, now, that's an elitist and chauvinistic view of "women," as if most women throughout human history, and most women in today's New York or Bogalusa, were whole, multifaceted, and intelligent persons, as if women in general were such awesome specimens of humanity that all men in their right minds would passionately desire to relate to them on a level beyond the sexual and despite what they look like. Yes, pornography focuses on the sexy parts, as does sex itself; but that it permits this distancing from the demands of relating to whole (and wholly decrepit) persons must also be a blessing, if it is a curse.

Another example is the claim that men's sexual interest in children and child pornography is fueled by the problems men have relating to mature women. In child pornography, says the political theorist Jean Elshtain, there "is a night-marish fantasy world in which the consumer . . . escapes the perils of adult intimacy in an era of changing sex roles."[41] In this regard, the philosopher Judith Bat-Ada pinpoints the magazine *Playboy*:

> Readers feel short-changed when a woman does not look and act the part of the *Playboy* model. . . . He cannot seem to attract the good-looking model in *Playboy*; instead he is stuck with a woman who has borne three children, gained weight, grown older with time. It makes him hate her. And it makes him turn to the younger female daughters in the family.[42]

For Bat-Ada, the man who is "stuck" with his older spouse (is this *his* punishment? his enormous suffering?) not only peruses *Playboy* for satisfying images of young girls, but is prepared or driven to engage in incest, in part led there by *Playboy*. Bat-Ada has no evidence for this projection of her fears. But, as we have seen with MacKinnon and Shrage, she is not the only feminist who fancies that she has privileged access to the minds of men, their sexuality, and how they conceive of pornography and their relation to it.

Consider, finally, Laura Lederer (a founder of Women Against Violence in Pornography and Media) and Diana Russell's version of Chesler's Complaint, which also attempts to explain the appeal of child pornography:

> We see this proliferation of pornography, especially violent pornography and child pornography, as part of the male backlash to the women's liberation movement. Enough women have been rejecting the traditional role of subordination to men to cause a crisis in the collective male ego. As women have become stronger and more assertive, some men find it easier to feel powerful with young girls, including children. Hence the enormous increase in child pornography in recent years.[43]

The last claim about the motivation of men who consume child pornography seems inconsistent with Lederer and Russell's claim that *child* pornography is backlash against women's liberation. If women are becoming more powerful, perhaps pornography in which adult women are bound and whipped can be understood as backlash against women, women's liberation, and feminism. But if men seek child pornography (or children) because it is now more difficult for them to be or feel powerful with adult women, child pornography represents a retreat from adult women, an admission of defeat. The content of run-of-the-mill child pornography provides no opportunity for men to get revenge in fantasy against feminist troublemakers or in fantasy to put rebellious adult women back in their places. Furthermore, Lederer and Russell are at best guessing, or pretending to be able to read the minds of men, when they claim that men compare liberated adult women with young girls and decide that feeling powerful with the former is hopeless and for this reason turn to youngsters. In the absence of serious psychological research, they fill in the blanks with their own fearsome female fantasy about men. Note the vague "some" men in the passage. Lederer and Russell can avoid the charge of mass-scale, outrageous, solipsistic "mind reading" by insisting that they are speaking only about *some* men. The smaller the number of men to whom they attribute these motivations, the more plausible their claim (it becomes trivially true). But if Lederer and Russell severely limit the number of men about whom they are speaking, their explanation for the "enormous increase" in child pornography collapses. (There really isn't that much, beyond the innocent photographs posted on the newsgroup alt.binaries.pictures.nudism.) To explain in these terms the purportedly large output of that industry, Lederer and Russell must assume that a huge number of men have these motivations. That proposition would be credible only to the gullible and the paranoid.

Soft Core and the Frenzy of the Visible Panty Line

In her essay "Objectification," Martha Nussbaum criticizes *Playboy* on the grounds that it objectifies women, but she also offers against it a version of Chesler's Complaint. Among Nussbaum's six exhibits of sexual material, which she presents as candidates for objectifying depictions, she includes an item from *Playboy* (April 1995):

> (4.) Three pictures of actress Nicollette Sheridan playing at the Chris Evert Pro-Celebrity Tennis Classic, her skirt hiked up to reveal her black underpants. Caption: "Why We Love Tennis."[44]

Here is Nussbaum's analysis:

> The *Playboy* caption reduces the young actress, a skilled tennis player, to a body ripe for male use: it says, in effect, she thinks she is displaying herself as a skilled athletic performer, but all the while she is actually displaying herself to *our* gaze as a sexual object.[45]

I don't see the "use": we are merely peeking up her skirt. Is looking at another person for the pleasure of doing so "using" them? Perhaps, if we stretch that concept.[46] Note that the phrase, "her skirt hiked up," is part of Nussbaum's own description of the photograph, her own caption. Who did this hiking up? Nussbaum unintentionally attributes agency to Sheridan here, as if the actress were playing on the power of her ass. If Sheridan did the hiking, who is using whom?

Even so, Nussbaum is making a sex-crime mountain out of a sex-act molehill:

> [T]he male reader is told, in effect, that he is the one with subjectivity and autonomy, and on the other side are things that look very sexy and are displayed out there for his consumption, like delicious pieces of fruit, existing only or primarily to satisfy his desire.[47]

Never mind that a photograph of my paternal grandmother renders me subject and my captured Bubbie an object to be looked at for pleasure, to be consumed and "used."[48] Never mind that to be seen as a delicious piece of fruit, given the disgusting nature of humans, is flattery. What Nussbaum thinks is conveyed by the photograph and its caption is an awful lot to be "told" ("in effect," is her fudge) by photographs of this sort. Nussbaum, projecting into the minds of male viewers of *Playboy* who hear what is "told" and of those who do the telling, packs her favorite feminist phrases into that otherwise empty male mental space. While reading so many male minds, why couldn't she write, more reasonably or sympathetically, "existing only or primarily—at this one brief moment, but not for eternity—to satisfy his innocuous desire"? For Nussbaum acknowledges in another context that we may rightfully treat others as objects some of the time. Objectification, according to Nussbaum, is inherent in sex; still, sexual objectification that occurs "in the moment of lovemaking" is acceptable, she says, since it "can be and frequently is accompanied by an intense concern for the subjectivity of the partner at other moments."[49] On such a calculus, according to which one may treat another person as an object at one time as long as one treats that other person with full dignity and respect at other times, all that voyeurs of Ms. Sheridan's rump need to do, to be treating her as a whole, multifaceted person, is to admire her tremendous tennis or acting skills at other times. On the other hand, perhaps these voyeurs cannot satisfy Nussbaum's test for permissible objectification, for it is unlikely (although not impossible) that they have "intense concern" for Ms. Sheridan's "subjectivity" beyond or outside the context of inspecting her backside. But if having this sort of intermittent intense concern for another person is a requirement of permissibly objectifying that person during sexual activity, Nussbaum has neatly condemned all casual sexual encounters, for in these events it is equally unlikely that the two parties have intense concern for each other. If sexual objectification cannot be attenuated without the formation of close intimate bonds, and sexual objectification is taken to be morally repulsive, not only are casual sex and the voyeurism made possible by *Playboy* morally wrong, but almost everything else. The conservative strain in Nussbaum's feminism is alarmingly clear.[50]

Nussbaum's reading of *Playboy* sounds extraordinarily familiar and stale, even though it was penned in the mid-1990s:

The message given by picture and caption is, "whatever else this woman is and does, for us she is an object for sexual enjoyment." . . . [W]hat *Playboy* repeatedly says to its readers is, Whoever this woman is and whatever she has achieved, for you she is cunt.[51]

Again, while reading men's minds, why couldn't Nussbaum more reasonably or sympathetically write, "she is, in addition to whatever else she is, an object for sexual enjoyment"? For about her own brand of acceptable sexual objectification, she says: "The intense focusing of attention on the bodily parts seems an addition, rather than a subtraction."[52] Nussbaum's interpretation of her *Playboy* exhibit utterly lacks imagination; it merely re-mouths a very old feminist line on the magazine.[53] Had she taken a look at *Hustler* and read Laura Kipnis, Nussbaum might have been able to come up with a more interesting reading of an item in which *Playboy* encroaches on *Hustler*'s turf. *Playboy* and its viewers are owning up to Nicollette Sheridan's fake, silly celebrity status: "Nicollette, you have been manufactured and foisted on us by the TV industry; you are no better—and no worse—than the rest of us schmucks; you are a nothing of an actress, a nobody, a flash in the pan, and certainly not a 'skilled tennis player,' as you and Nussbaum pretend; it therefore gives us pleasure to reduce you to a more appropriate status, to pull you down from the artificial pedestal upon which you bleat and boast; with the help of *Playboy*, however, you have salvaged something of worth, you can bask in the fact that you have a powerful, even if sweaty, panty-clad ass." Nussbaum is big on women, just because they are women, giving them credit where no credit is due. What Nicollette Sheridan "has achieved," indeed: she is the admirable renaissance woman who has a powerful backhand in tennis, is powerful as an actress, *and* sports that powerful ass. Nicollette Sheridan, a mental *hors de combat*, chases the bitch-goddess, Success. That Nussbaum is big on Sheridan tells us more about Nussbaum's own embarrassing values than about Sheridan. Nussbaum ends the "cunt" sentence with "all her pretensions vanish before your sexual power,"[54] but she doesn't take seriously the viewer's idea that Sheridan's "pretensions" are in fact just pretensions. Nor is she right to think that these pretensions collapse, in the viewer's mind, through his imagined "sexual power." Do the viewers imagine that they are handsome dudes? That they have the power of the male? An unsubtle Nussbaum forces men to be the stereotypes that much of feminism makes them out to be. Men are lucky to be able to use their minimal economic power to catch a foggy glimpse of Sheridan's rear end, which is something they know while masturbating with *Playboy*—instead of using their sexual power to "get" or "possess" a real woman.

It would have been more persuasive for Nussbaum to select as an example a woman who has genuine talent. But that tactic would also fail to substantiate her point. Suppose that I am in the audience during the Hungarian chess championship, watching Polgár Judit beat the pants off the Magyar men at a (traditionally) man's game. I am in awe as I watch her moves displayed by an overhead projector, thrilled by her brilliance. Her opponent in this game is now thinking for a long time in a difficult position. My eyes wander from the projection to Judit, to her feminine form sitting on the stage at the Hotel Béke. My eyes move slowly, delicately and deliciously, from her long, flowing hair down to her legs, plenty of succulent thigh exposed by her short, tight skirt, and I fasten, finally, on the hint of bulging buttock, slightly flattened by her hard chair. "Oh! to be that chair!" (Or, as in Lawrence: "if I only lived ten minutes, an' stroked thy arse an' got to know it, I should reckon I'd lived *one* life, see ter!") I then think to myself, "Why I love chess." Clearly, this is a self-critical *joke*, which Nussbaum misses in her dreadfully solemn analysis of the *Playboy* caption, "Why we love tennis."[55] Have I used Judit? Have I demeaned her? Have I exerted my male power over her? Or have I found in her multifaceted existence yet another attractive dimension? It doesn't matter; nothing to get morally hot and bothered about has occurred in my demented mind. Or take Nussbaum delivering one of her many well-attended lectures at a meeting of the American Philosophical Association. I listen carefully to her well-chosen, erudite words, and I easily perceive the beauty of her presentation (the way Socrates was attuned to the beauty of Agathon's speech in the *Symposium*). Not only that. During a slow section of her paper, I allow my eyes to move gracefully down her body, inspecting her curves and dress and imagining what lies beneath. "Why I love philosophy" is what I sardonically console myself with for having committed myself to sitting through the whole thing. Or consider the female pianist I am sitting behind on the left side of the orchestra. Her performance of the Mozart rondo is spectacular, I enjoy it immensely, and admire her ability. But inveterate I cannot keep either eye off a backside encased in tight slacks. "Why I love the piano," I joke to myself. After her last piece (or *as* her last piece), the pianist—of course—bends over. The polysemicity of her music is still ringing in my ears as I appreciate the polysemicity of this kind gesture. Women, too, don't have a pure interest in the ballet of basketball or the ferocity and finesses of football. Biceps and buns galore also partially explain why women love these sports. Check out Baryshnikov's bulging crotch and you may gain a new appreciation of a woman's (or man's) "love" of ballet.

Perhaps sensing, even while writing it, that her analysis of *Playboy* as objectifying women wouldn't fly, Nussbaum raises against the magazine a version of Chesler's Complaint, about which she says, "One may accept this criticism of *Playboy* even if one is not convinced that its portrayal of women is sufficiently depersonalizing to count as objectification."[56] This is how the criticism goes: "Used as a masturbatory aid, it [*Playboy*] encourages the idea that an easy satisfaction can be had in this uncomplicated way, without the difficulties attendant on recognizing women's subjectivity and autonomy in a more full-blooded way."[57] Sure, it *is* more difficult to maintain a relationship with a real human being; that seems to be a corollary of general misanthropy, if I might use Nussbaum's remark to my own advantage. But Nussbaum seems to assume that having full-bodied relationships is an obligation, or is a mode of existence morally superior to casual sex, or that, in comparison with a life of cold fucks or solitary masturbation with pornography, being coupled and working damn hard at it is more suitable to the dignity of the human being. This unexamined prejudice in favor of the difficult coupled life over many other sexual lifestyles emerges quietly in several tiny passages of her wordy, pretentious essay. Nussbaum condemns, sounding like Pope John Paul II, the principle of heterosexual casual sex: "*Playboy* depicts a thoroughgoing fungibility and commodification of sex partners, and, in the process, severs sex from any deep connection with self-expression or emotion."[58] Also unacceptably objectifying is gay male promiscuity, about which Nussbaum says, sounding like her nemesis, the philosopher and legal scholar John Finnis,[59]

> [I]n the absence of any narrative history with the person, how can desire attend to anything else but the incidental, and how can one do more than use the body of the other as a tool of one's own state?[60]

> Can one really treat someone with the respect and concern that democracy requires if one has sex with him in the anonymous spirit?[61]

Now we can see why Nussbaum noneuphemistically refers to the "moment of lovemaking." She was not talking about casual sex or cold fucking. This mature professor, like a sexually protected young girl, cannot fathom that such things are within the bounds of perfectly unobjectionable human conduct. With yet another (former!) nemesis of hers, Roger Scruton, Nussbaum implicitly agrees that "[t]he ideal of virtue remains one of 'sexual integrity': of a sexuality that is entirely integrated into the life of personal affection."[62] Of course, it is an intriguing, perplexing question, why human beings want relationships with other human beings. But the "desire for intimacy" answer (to overcome existential Angst?) may involve prodigious illusions about the quality of our close ties; not every couple is an Iris Murdoch and John Bayles, since intimacy breeds as much contempt and hatred as it does sympathy. The "desire for sexual satisfaction" (period), whether it comes with or without Nussbaumian-Scrutonian "integration," has just as much claim to being the real story, and is more consistent with the sexual worldview expressed in pornography.

MacKinnon's take on *Playboy*, in contrast to Nussbaum's anachronisms, is refreshing in its imaginative, original inanity:

> Behaviorally, *Playboy*'s consumers are reading about the First Amendment, masturbating to the women, reading about the First Amendment, masturbating to the women, reading about the First Amendment, masturbating to the women. It makes subliminal seduction look subtle. What is conveyed is not only that using women is as legitimate as thinking about the Constitution, but also that if you don't support these views about the Constitution, you won't be able to use these women.[63]

While she is doing this sophisticated and profound associationistic psychology, MacKinnon might as well conclude that by masturbating to the women's photographs as they page through the magazine, men will come to find the dry language of the Constitution as sexy as the automobiles and sound systems profusely advertised in *Playboy*. MacKinnon's view of "what is conveyed" by the magazine is as poor and as paranoid a reading of *Playboy* as Nussbaum's view of what "the male reader is told" by *Playboy*. MacKinnon and Nussbaum are unsympathetically guessing, projecting, and provide not a shred of evidence that this *is* what is conveyed or told or registers in the minds of male viewers. Referring to the definition of pornography in her antipornography Ordinance, MacKinnon claims—unwilling to make fine distinctions—that

> [t]his definition [of pornography as the subordination of women] is coterminous with the industry, from *Playboy*, in which women are objectified and presented dehumanized as sexual objects or things for use; through the torture of women and the sexualization of racism and the fetishization of women's body parts to snuff films, in which actual murder is the ultimate sexual act.[64]

We saw earlier that Nicholas Lemann aligned defecation with mutilation, in his outrage at prostitution in old New Orleans. Aligning *Playboy* with the apocryphal snuff film and the worst sadomasochistic pornography, as if each were located close to each other on the same continuum, is just as peculiar. It is to call a minor, innocuous piece of photographic objectification—Nicollette's revealed ass—the same kind of thing as the brutal beating of unwilling women. Nussbaum explicitly registers her agreement "with MacKinnon and Dworkin, who have repeatedly stressed the essential similarity between the soft-core and the hard-core pornography industries."[65] (There is more MacKinnon worship in Nussbaum: "Kant, MacKinnon, and Dworkin are correct in one central insight: that the instrumental treatment of human beings, the treatment of human beings as tools of the purposes of another, is always morally problematic; if it does not take place in a larger context of regard for humanity, it is a central form of the morally objectionable."[66] Are correct? Says who? Well, Kant, MacKinnon, Dworkin, Nussbaum, and Pope John Paul II. I'm not impressed. Distinguished, multidepartment Chicago professors and presidents of the American Philosophical Association, Central Division, also cherish their illusions.) Even if the tactic of conflating *Playboy* with snuff films stirs up feminist rage against pornography and promises to draw otherwise neutral women into the battle against it, the maneuver is intellectually sloppy. Categorizing mild sexual harassment—an offensive sexist remark—as yet another kind of sexual assault or rape is just as sloppy. The fact that *Playboy*, on MacKinnon's account, falls within the terms of her Ordinance strongly suggests that "normal" male heterosexuality, and the *eros* and objectification of sex itself, not brutally violent pornography, are the objects of her attack.

MacKinnon trashes *Playboy* and other American pornography, but I have never found a word of hers that specifically condemns the particulars of Japanese pornography. If MacKinnon were willing to make the distinctions she eschews, and to do a thorough (not cursory) job of documenting, on her view, the worst features of pornography worldwide, her message would be less inane. But MacKinnon, in her determination to encourage women to bring suit against the American *Playboy*, of all things, did not stop to investigate and exhibit Japanese pornography. Pornography produced in Japan, and easily available in the United States, contains a great deal of realistically staged male-dominant sadomasochism; Japan permits the dissemination of photographs of very young nude girls, photographs that in the States and by MacKinnon would be considered kiddie porn; and Japanese pornography unabashedly displays young, attractive, well-dressed girls urinating and defecating, eating and barfing, and, in "bukkake" photographs, taking jumbo loads of ejaculate, from several penises, on their faces. (Browse the Web site www.giga-jp.com and the newsgroup alt.binaries.pictures.erotica.orientals.) Even if I don't consider all this pornography revolting or objectionable, MacKinnon surely does, and why she would pass up such a choice opportunity to beef up her attack by revealing the nature of Japanese pornography is a small mystery—unless she finds it embarrassing to her thesis about the harmful causal effects of pornography that Japan, despite the kind of pornography to be found in abundance there, has a low incidence of rape.[67] Or is she afraid of being accused of antioriental racism or of Japan bashing, which is less popular than *Playboy* bashing? Maybe MacKinnon, despite promoting herself as an expert on the subject, hasn't taken a very good look at the whole world of pornography. You'd think someone with legislative goals would have done her homework.

THE LOVE GAMBIT

Nussbaum's reference to "lovemaking," which was not at all meant as a polite euphemism, gives her game away. The objectification that is essential to sexual congress cannot, for Nussbaum, be purified or made agreeable in casual sex, but only in relationships that have a "narrative history" and in which the people have an "intense concern" for each other's "subjectivity." This intimate, narrative history and its accompanying focus on the "subjectivity" of the partners is what men fear and flee, according to Chesler. So Nussbaum's feminism, which requires that sex occur within the intimate nexus of a relationship, is "in effect" an unmodified feminism, in the sense of one-sidedly supporting women's interests in intimacy against men's interests in detachment, cold sex, pornography, and prostitution.[68] Lawrence's solution, if he was even attempting to solve the sexual objectification problem, seems to be "fucking with a warm heart."[69] Again, no cold fucks.

The reluctance to countenance casual sex in Nussbaum is symptomatic of two related trends in feminist antipornography writings: they are antisexual and they are sexually naive. Literature professor Jane Gallop's offhand remark doesn't face up to this:

> In the 1980s feminists targeted pornography and created a revival of feminism as a movement with wide social influence. In the 1990s, sexual harassment has replaced pornography as the high-profile feminist issue. Like pornography, harassment allows feminists to reach a broad audience. Like pornography, the focus on harassment runs the risk of being widely misunderstood as an objection to sexuality rather than sexism.[70]

Feminist critiques of pornography are not "misunderstood" as being antisexual. They *are* antisexual. This is illustrated by Nussbaum on casual sex, both heterosexual and homosexual. The "dehumanization" objection raised against pornography by Russell, Itzin, and the others I have discussed are also antisexual: to claim that some harmless sexual acts and their depictions (ejaculation, fellatio, urination, defecation, anal intercourse) are degrading, and not even consent suffices to redeem them, implies that some kinds of sexuality, of a sort disliked by these writers, not just sexism, is the object of attack. Both the feminist and the conservative attack on pornography are informed by a nifty, and probably true, equation: It is permissible to make an image of a sexual act if and only if it is permissible to do that act, or it is wrong to make an image of a sexual act if and only if it is wrong to engage in that act. Their narrow judgments as to what is permissible in pornography derive, then, from their narrow judgments of what it is permissible to *do* sexually.

MacKinnon and Dworkin, in well-known passages, provide other examples of feminist antisexualism. MacKinnon: "In pornography, the penis is shown ramming up into the woman over and over; this is because it actually was rammed up into the woman over and over. . . . No pornography is 'real' sex in the sense of shared intimacy; this may make it a lie, but it does not make it 'simulated.'"[71] MacKinnon's prejudice contrasts "ramming" with "shared intimacy." Dworkin offers her own version of "ramming." In intercourse, she writes,

> female is bottom, stigmatized. Intercourse remains a means or the means of physiologically making a woman inferior: communicating to her cell by cell her own inferior status, impressing it on her, burning it into her by shoving it into her, over and over, pushing and thrusting until she gives up and gives in.[72]

And men should "give up their precious erections and begin to make love as women do together."[73] Heterosex, without more, is the culprit. I doubt, then, that Gallop would be right to assert that the Freud scholar Leo Bersani has "misunderstood" unmodified feminism:

> The ultimate logic of MacKinnon's and Dworkin's critique of pornography . . . would be *the criminalization of sex itself until it has been reinvented.* For their most radical claim is not that pornography has a pernicious effect on otherwise nonpernicious sexual relations, but rather that so-called normal sexuality is already pornographic.[74]

Even a feminist legal scholar who rejects MacKinnon's radical line on heterosexuality and who wants to provide a moderate alternative to unmodified feminism gets caught up in her own sexual absurdity. According to Ruth Colker,

"Feminism aspires to assist us [to] come closer to discovering and experiencing our authentic selves."[75] One dimension of authenticity, for Colker, is "authentic sexuality," which "refers to the loving connectedness that we would choose to share with others as well as ourselves if we could fully glimpse our authentic selves."[76] What a homey connection between sex and love! Colker proceeds to reveal its downside: "I have been involved in intimate sexual relationships with both men and women but have never experienced a relationship that seemed fully authentic to me. I have, therefore, often wondered what I would discover if I could get in touch with my authentic sexuality."[77] Colker's diagnosis for the failure of her sexual and loving relationships is that her (or the) deep, authentic self is elusive. I would have thought: good sexual and loving relationships are rare because people are disgusting, especially at their so-called deeper levels. (For Aristotle, genuine friendship is rare because good men are few and far between.)[78] Colker's illusion is that there is a deep, authentic self; looking for something that doesn't exist, she has of course never experienced what she has convinced herself she should be experiencing.

Let us turn, finally, to a feminist classic on sex and love, Robin Morgan's claim that "rape exists any time sexual intercourse occurs when it has not been initiated by the woman, out of her own genuine affection and desire."[79] A necessary condition for heterosexual intercourse not to be rape is that the event is initiated by the woman, and she must initiate the event for two reasons (motives), "out of" her affection (something akin to love) and her own sexual desire. Any other motives for the event on the woman's part make heterosexual coitus rape. Morgan's notion of rape condemns prostitution, casual sex, star-fucking, playful group sex, and, of course, a woman's participating in the production of pornography. Further, as she concludes, "under this definition, most of the decently married bedrooms across America are settings for nightly rape."[80] Women, apparently, do not initiate marital sexual activity often enough for Morgan, or when they do initiate marital sex they do so for suspicious reasons. Under the influence of Morganian thinking, Diana Russell discusses the pornographic use of video technology:

> As an increasing number of Americans . . . own . . . video cameras, more men are making their own pornographic home movies. It would be interesting to know in what percentage of cases women *initiate* the making of such videos and decide on the content. Of these women, it would also be relevant to find out . . . what proportion desire such videos for themselves, in contrast to trying to please their male partners.[81]

Russell implies that if the man or the husband proposes to set up the video camera on a tripod in the bedroom, the woman or his wife is merely being used. Or she participates in the making of the tape just to please him, not having any interest in that sort of enterprise herself. Both scenarios are repugnant to Russell. Her alternative, acceptable scenario would involve the woman initiating the making of the tape and her being its director, deciding on its content, what activities they perform in front of the camera. But one can agree with Russell that for women to take a more active role in the production of pornographic home videos is commendable, without going whole hog with her and complaining that when women participate just to please their men, something objectionable is going on. Perhaps Russell and Morgan assume that if a woman does something sexual for her man simply out of a desire to please him, she is expressing the self-sacrificing behavior she has been conditioned to express. That thesis is much too strong; it eliminates any possibility that caring on the part of women is ever genuine. At any rate,

Russell's proposal is odd, given her immoderate critique of the degrading nature of pornography. She allows here that the home production of pornography is unobjectionable were the woman to initiate its making and to decide its content. But what if the woman desired to film her husband's ejaculating on her face? Or her husband's penetrating her anally? In her proposal, Russell has embraced a procedural criterion of acceptable sexual material, rather than a content-based criterion. I think that a procedural criterion has great merit, but it is inconsistent with Russell's attempt to provide a list of the sexual activities in pornography that are objectively degrading.

Morgan's definition of rape, if taken literally, also condemns any intercourse in which there *is* affection, but the affection is not the woman's *motive*. Morgan's definition of rape rules out intercourse initiated by the woman, in which the two people express affection for each other, but the affection was not the woman's reason for engaging in the act—her motive, say, was just horniness or to give pleasure to her partner. Who is to say that Morgan did not intend this absurd consequence? To argue that this consequence was not intended, because it is absurd, is to forget that her definition is already absurd, according to which most households are the location of nightly rapes. Besides, not to take Morgan at her own apparently carefully chosen word, to forbid her from multiplying absurdities as she sees fit, would be to patronize her, a woman, and no one should commit that paramount sin of sexism. This sort of feminist antisexualism, along with the choice parts of the MacKinnon-Dworkin corpus, has given unmodified feminism, and the rest of it by guilty association, a bad name. But unmodified feminism is too popular among academic feminists to be ignored or written off as (which it is) the incoherent rants of a lunatic fringe. It trickles down from fanatic feminist professors to their more gullible and surly female students, and spreads like an infection into the philosophy of science.[82]

Dworkin has exuberantly endorsed Morgan's definition of rape, putting a historical spin on it:

> Intercourse not willed and initiated by the woman was rape, in [Victoria] Woodhull's analysis. She anticipated current feminist critiques of intercourse—modest and rare as they are—by a century. As if to celebrate the centennial of Woodhull's repudiation of male-supremacist sexual intercourse, Robin Morgan in 1974 transformed Woodhull's insight into a firm principle: *"I claim that rape exists any time sexual intercourse occurs when it has not been initiated by the woman, out of her own genuine affection and desire."*[83]

Morgan's definition, according to Dworkin, derives from another great, early feminist, Victoria Woodhull. In *Intercourse*, Dworkin praises Woodhull's Morganism:

> The great advocate of the female-first model of intercourse in the nineteenth-century was Victoria Woodhull. . . . [W]omen had a *natural* right—a right that inhered in the nature of intercourse itself—to be entirely self-determining, the controlling and dominating partner, the one whose desire determined the event, the one who both initiates and is the final authority on what the sex is and will be. . . . [T]he only condition under which women could experience sexual freedom in intercourse—real choice, real freedom, real happiness, real pleasure—was in having real and absolute control in each and every act of intercourse, which would be, each and every time, chosen by the woman.[84]

To support her reading, Dworkin quotes this passage from Woodhull's "Tried as by Fire":

To woman, by nature, belongs the right of sexual determination. When the instinct is aroused in her, then and then
only should commerce follow. When woman rises from
sexual slavery to sexual freedom, into the ownership and
control of her sexual organs, and man is obliged to respect
this freedom, then will this instinct become pure and holy;
then will woman be raised from the iniquity and morbid-
ness in which she now wallows for existence, and the
intensity and glory of her creative functions can be
increased a hundred-fold.[85]

Dworkin immediately comments: "The consent standard
is revealed as pallid, weak, stupid, second-class, by contrast
with Woodhull's standard: that the woman should have
authority and control over the act."[86] But Dworkin does not
pause to wonder about Woodhull's phrase "her creative functions." Dworkin, more a polemicist than a trustworthy
scholar, sacrifices historical and textual accuracy for the political usefulness of a few isolated quotations. What Woodhull
really said, conveniently ignored by Dworkin, was that sexual
intercourse should be initiated by the woman, and should
occur only with a man she loves and desires, *because* coitus in
those conditions would produce the most healthy offspring.
Woman's "real choice, real freedom, real happiness, real pleasure" in sexuality are, according to Woodhull, necessary precisely for the sake of her progeny and her reproductive
"divinity." Consider these choice lines from Woodhull's pen:

And my sisters. Oh! what shall I say to them; how awaken
them to realize the awful responsibilities conferred through
their maternal functions. How shall I arouse, how startle
them, into a comprehension of the divinity of maternity?

[A] woman who bears a dozen or less scraggy, scrawny,
puny, half-made-up children, by a legal father, is a disgrace

to her sex and a curse to the community; while she who bears as many perfect specimens of humanity, no matter if it be by as many different fathers, is an honor to woman-hood and a blessing to the world.

Women cannot bear their best children except by the men they love best and for whom they have the keenest desire.

Sexual freedom . . . means the birth of love-children only, endowed by every inherited virtue that the highest exalta-tion can confer at conception, by every influence for good to be obtained during gestation.

I protest against this form of slavery, I *protest* against the custom which compels women to give the control of their maternal functions over to anybody. It should be *theirs* to determine *when*, and under what circumstances, the greatest of all constructive processes—the formation of an immortal soul—should be begun.[87]

There is not much second-wave feminism here, or any kind of recognizable feminism. To defend women's sexual rights on the grounds of the necessity of producing the best pos-sible children in heterosexual intercourse, is to imprison women in their reproductive role, not to free them from it. And it makes women's sexual pleasure ancillary and subor-dinate to their destiny as child bearers—a nice piece of con-servative philosophy that contemporary feminists usually condemn as supportive of the patriarchy.

Leaving Woodhull behind, why does Morgan, for her part, want sexual intercourse to occur only out of the woman's own genuine desire and affection? Morgan is wor-ried, as is Catherine Itzin, that otherwise the woman will be coerced, forced into sex, pressured, since she is in patriarchy the social and sexual subordinate of the male. But Morgan's definition of acceptable, nonrape sex does not make women free. Insisting that a woman engage in intercourse only out of her own affection and desire (instead of, say, for the money or the hell of it) makes or leaves the woman a slave, no longer in control, in the same way that men lose power to the women they desire and feel affection for. There is nothing, except extreme economic need, that undermines one's sexual autonomy as much as being compelled or propelled by the combination of sexual desire and "genuine" affection for the object of one's attention. (This factor might contribute to the equality of the relationship between Connie Chatterley and Oliver Mellors: it is not that her aristocracy is balanced by his male privilege, but that her sexual desire for him reduces her power.) The irony is that in seeking sexual freedom for women, rather too easily in women's initiating coitus, Morgan's feminism utilizes that which makes anyone a slave. Casual sex, even a cold fuck, even a bought fuck, is less a threat to one's autonomy. Not to do it out of one's own subordinating desire is to escape bondage; to be indifferent or purely pragmatic is to be free. When Margaret Jean Intons-Peterson and Beverly Roskos-Ewoldsen (a psychology professor and her student) condemn pornography because "[w]omen are the slaves, the sexual playthings, for men to use and discard. . . . Their chief interest is the satisfaction of male sexual desire,"[88] they, too, overlook that were women concerned, instead, with the satisfaction of their own sexual desire, not the male's, they would still be slaves, perhaps more ruthlessly so. As Augustine saw, to be unperturbed by sexual desire (*per impossibile*, for him, in the postlapsarian world) would be to be free. Women who participate in the making of pornography neither out of severe economic need nor out of their own sexual desire and affection, and who thereby engage in these sexual acts coldly, without emotional entanglements, and do them for the pragmatic reason that they prefer this job, with its good pay, to the poorly paying jobs in fast-food restaurants they could have had—are free. Good for them. Only the moralist conservative and the maternalist feminist worry about her leasing her body in this way instead of some other way.

The freedom to choose one's reasons for engaging in sex is an important part of sexual freedom. To claim, with Morgan, that women (to avoid being raped) must engage in sex only for some proper reason—out of their own affection and desire—but for no other reason at all, is to undermine the very freedom of women that Morgan and other feminists would like to promote. We used to call this kind of meddling interference with the motives and choices and lives of people "fascism" or "totalitarianism." Morgan's philosophy, in ruling out a whole slew of sexual possibilities for women, dominates women by purporting to be freeing them. This is not a new phenomenon. As Connie Chatterley exclaimed, "Now . . . she was free of the domination of *other women*. Ah! that in itself was a relief, like being given another life."[89]

NOTES

1. Naomi Wolf, *The Beauty Myth: How Images of Beauty Are Used Against Women* (New York: Doubleday, 1992), p. 145.

2. Diana E. H. Russell, "Introduction," in *Making Violence Sexy: Feminist Views on Pornography*, ed. Diana E. H. Russell (New York: Teachers College Press, 1993), p. 15.

3. Lillian B. Rubin, *Erotic Wars: What Happened to the Sexual Revolution?* (New York: Farrar, Straus and Giroux, 1990), p. 128.

4. Ibid., p. 129.

5. See my critique of some of Rae Langton's writings on pornography, in my "Bad Apples: Feminist Politics and Feminist Scholarship," *Philosophy of the Social Sciences* 29, no. 3 (1999): 354–88.

6. Catherine Itzin, "Introduction: Fact, Fiction and Faction,"

in *Pornography: Women, Violence and Civil Liberties*, ed. Catherine Itzin (Oxford: Oxford University Press, 1992), p. 10.

7. Cynthia A. Stark, "Is Pornography an Action?: The Causal vs. the Conceptual View of Pornography's Harm," *Social Theory and Practice* 23, no. 2 (1997): 303 n. 10.

8. Diana E. H. Russell, "Pornography and Violence: What Does the New Research Say?" in *Take Back the Night: Women on Pornography*, ed. Laura Lederer (New York: William Morrow, 1980), p. 224.

9. For uncritical, mechanical deployments of Russell's data, see John Stoltenberg, *Refusing To Be a Man: Essays on Sex and Justice* (Portland, Ore.: Breitenbush Books, 1989), pp. 149-50; and Hollis Wheeler, "Pornography and Rape: A Feminist Perspective," in *Rape and Sexual Assault: A Research Handbook*, ed. Ann Wolbert Burgess (New York: Garland, 1985), pp. 383–85.

10. Pauline Bart, "Testimony in the Los Angeles Hearing (1985)," in *In Harm's Way: The Pornography Civil Rights Hearings*, ed. Catharine A. MacKinnon and Andrea Dworkin (Cambridge: Harvard University Press, 1997), p. 343.

11. Dolf Zillmann and Jennings Bryant, "Pornography, Sexual Callousness, and the Trivialization of Rape," *Journal of Communication* 32, no. 4 (1982): 12, italics added; see also pp. 19-20.

12. Russell, "Pornography and Violence," p. 228.

13. See Daphne Patai, *Heterophobia: Sexual Harassment and the Future of Feminism* (Lanham, Md.: Rowman and Littlefield, 1998), pp. 27, 39.

14. Charlene Y. Senn, "The Research on Women and Pornography: The Many Faces of Harm," in *Making Violence Sexy: Feminist Views on Pornography*, ed. Diana E. H. Russell (New York: Teachers College Press, 1993), pp. 188–89.

15. Ibid., p. 193.

16. Lillian B. Rubin, *Intimate Strangers: Men and Women Together* (New York: Harper and Row, 1983); see the excerpt, "Women, Men, and Intimacy," in *Eros, Agape, and Philia: Readings in the Philosophy of Love*, ed. Alan Soble (St. Paul, Minn.: Paragon House, 1989), pp. 12–28.

17. There are some exceptions: the Web site "Dr. Bob's Scans"

(www.DBScans.com) and the magazine *Over 40*. In another essay, Chesler is more accurate: "Few pornographic fantasies involve 'older' women as the desirable sexual objects" ("Men and Pornography: Why They Use It," in *Take Back the Night: Women on Pornography*, ed. Laura Lederer [New York: William Morrow, 1980], p. 157).

18. Phyllis Chesler, "Opening Statement," in "Panel Discussion: Effects of Violent Pornography," *New York University Review of Law and Social Change* 8, no. 2 (1978–79): 231.

19. Morgan is certain that men's wandering is caused by pornography. About "the effects of pornography," she says, "some obvious trends can be noted: . . . the promotion of infidelity and betrayal as a swinging alternative to committed relationships" ("Theory and Practice: Pornography and Rape," in *Going Too Far: The Personal Chronicle of a Feminist* [New York: Random House, 1977], p. 168). As if men didn't wander plenty before and without pornography, and women, too—out of their own genuine affection and desire. Dolf Zillmann and Jennings Bryant are more circumspect than Morgan:

> [R]epeated exposure to pornography prompted respondents to consider recreational sexual engagements without any emotional involvement or attachment increasingly important. . . . [I]t is important to note that the impact of pornography consumption is not gender-specific. Sexual dissatisfaction befell women just as strongly as it befell men.

"Pornography's Impact on Sexual Satisfaction," *Journal of Applied Social Psychology* 18, no. 5 (1988): 450.

20. Phyllis Chesler, "Letter, December 7, 1983 (Exhibit 13 [44] in The Minneapolis Hearings)," in *In Harm's Way: The Pornography Civil Rights Hearings*, ed. Catharine A. MacKinnon and Andrea Dworkin (Cambridge: Harvard University Press, 1997), p. 228.

21. In contrast to Chesler, Robin West thinks women have too much sex with their men, instead of too little:

> [S]ome women occasionally, and many women quite frequently, consent to sex even when they do not desire the sex itself, and accordingly have a good deal of sex that, although consensual, is in no way pleasurable.

"The Harms of Consensual Sex," in *The Philosophy of Sex: Contemporary Readings*, 3rd ed., ed. Alan Soble (Lanham, Md.: Rowman and Littlefield, 1997), p. 263. West's loose expressions, especially "many women frequently," beg for hard and reliable statistics.

22. Chesler, "Men and Pornography," p. 156.

23. Chesler, "Opening Statement," p. 232.

24. Dolf Zillmann and Jennings Bryant, "Effects of Massive Exposure to Pornography," in *Pornography and Sexual Aggression*, ed. Neil M. Malamuth and Edward Donnerstein (Orlando, Fla.: Academic Press, 1984), p. 35.

25. Dolf Zillmann, *Connections between Sex and Aggression* (Hillsdale, N.J.: Lawrence Erlbaum, 1984), p. 193.

26. Ibid., p. 197.

27. Roger Scruton, *Sexual Desire: A Moral Philosophy of the Erotic* (New York: Free Press, 1986), p. 314; see p. 244.

28. See my *The Philosophy of Sex and Love: An Introduction* (St. Paul, Minn.: Paragon House, 1998), pp. 169–78, 183–84. For the idea that keeping pornography out of a relationship, instead of employing it, attenuates excitatory habituation, see Daniel Linz and Neil Malamuth, *Pornography* (Newbury Park, Calif.: Sage Publications, 1993), pp. 23–24.

29. Zillmann, *Connections*, p. 198.

30. Camille Paglia, *Sex, Art, and American Culture* (New York: Vintage, 1992), pp. 24-25.

31. Scruton, *Sexual Desire*, p. 345.

32. Andrea Dworkin, *Life and Death* (New York: Free Press, 1997), p. 140.

33. The passage from Dworkin immediately continues: "The minute you move away from what it really is, you move away from prostitution into the world of ideas." I think the proper reply to Dworkin is that when one is under the ideological spell of a certain sort of feminism, one ends up falsely attributing to the prostitute-client relationship all the horrors that *must of course* be there.

34. "The whore does not sell her body. She sells her time. So she has time that is not for sale, that belongs to no one but herself. Domesticated women don't dare put a price on their time . . . so

they have no time and space of their own. . . . [I]t's the john who has to give something away to the whore. He must tell her his secret desire if he is to get his money's worth. The whore in turn gives nothing away, laughs at him while she keeps her secrets and pockets his cash" (Pat Califia, *Macho Sluts* [Los Angeles, Calif.: Alyson Books, 1988], p. 20).

35. Laura Kipnis, *Bound and Gagged: Pornography and the Politics of Fantasy in America* (New York: Grove Press, 1996), pp. 199–200. See also her "(Male) Desire and (Female) Disgust: Reading *Hustler*," in *Cultural Studies*, ed. Lawrence Grossberg, Cary Nelson, and Paula A. Treichler (New York: Routledge, 1992), p. 380; Ferrel M. Christensen, "Cultural and Ideological Bias in Pornography Research," *Philosophy of the Social Sciences* 20, no. 3 (1990): 355-57; Eric Hoffman, "Feminism, Pornography, and Law," *University of Pennsylvania Law Review* 133, no. 2 (1985): 527.

36. Roger Scruton would have us cling to our illusions about the transcendental value of the human person: "[W]e must all learn the delicate negotiations whereby to disentangle ourselves from the unsolicited attentions of others, without offending their self-respect, and one of the most important features of moral education consists in the acquisition of the control implied by this transaction" (*Sexual Desire*, p. 83).

37. This is the thesis that Linda Williams found in my book *Pornography: Marxism, Feminism, and the Future of Sexuality* (New Haven, Conn.: Yale University Press, 1986); see her review essay, "Sexual Politics: Strange Bedfellows," *In These Times* (October 29–November 4, 1986): 20.

38. D. H. Lawrence, *Lady Chatterley's Lover* (New York: New American Library, 1962), p. 189.

39. For example:

> John: Darling, might I insert my penis into you *per anum* tonight?
> Jill: No! What do you think?
> John: Oh, come on, darling. I'd really like it. Just try.
> Jill: No! And if you care for me, you won't ask again.
> John (to himself): And, if you cared for me, you'd let me.

40. Sara Diamond, "Pornography: Image and Reality," in *Women Against Censorship*, ed. Varda Burstyn (Vancouver, B.C.: Douglas and McIntyre, 1985), p. 43.

41. Jean Bethke Elshtain, "The New Porn Wars," *New Republic* (June 25, 1984): 19.

42. Laura Lederer, "'*Playboy* Isn't Playing,' An Interview with Judith Bat-Ada," in *Take Back the Night: Women on Pornography*, ed. Laura Lederer (New York: William Morrow, 1980), pp. 130–31.

43. Lederer and Russell, "Questions We Get Asked Most Often," in ibid., pp. 27-28. See also Wheeler, "Pornography and Rape," pp. 377–78.

44. Martha C. Nussbaum, "Objectification," in *The Philosophy of Sex: Contemporary Readings*, 3rd ed., ed. Alan Soble (Lanham, Md.: Rowman and Littlefield, 1997), p. 286. In the later version of this essay that appears in Nussbaum's collection *Sex and Social Justice* (New York: Oxford University Press, 1999), p. 216, the passage appears this way:

> Why we love tennis. (A caption for three pictures of actress Nicollette Sheridan playing at the Chris Evert Pro-Celebrity Tennis Classic, her skirt hiked up to reveal her black underpants, *Playboy*, April 1995)

Unless stated otherwise, references to Nussbaum's essay "Objectification" are to the earlier version in *The Philosophy of Sex*.

45. Ibid., p. 288.

46. See my *Sexual Investigations* (New York: New York University Press, 1996), p. 99.

47. Nussbaum, "Objectification," p. 308.

48. "Any and all image-making dehumanizes models to some degree; and to some degree humanizes the material—film, ink, paint, paper, canvas, clay, stone, whatever it may be" (Scott Tucker, "Gender, Fucking, and Utopia," *Social Text* #27 [1990]: 3). See also my 1986 *Pornography* (p. 119) and my "Review of Susanne Kappeler's *The Pornography of Representation*," *Philosophy of the Social Sciences* 19, no. 1 (1989): 128–31.

49. Nussbaum, "Objectification," p. 303.

50. For more on Nussbaum, see my "Sexual Use and What to

Do about It: Internalist and Externalist Sexual Ethics," *Essays in Philosophy* 2, no. 2 (2001), at www.humboldt.edu/~essays/soble. html; a revised and expanded version can be found in my *The Philosophy of Sex*, 4th ed. (Lanham, Md.: Rowman and Littlefield, 2002), or at www.uno.edu/~asoble/pages/sexuse.htm.

51. Nussbaum, "Objectification," pp. 308, 310. This is the passage from the later version of "Objectification":

> The message given by the picture and the caption is, Whatever else this woman is and does, for us she is an object for sexual enjoyment.

Nussbaum, *Sex and Social Justice*, p. 234.

52. Nussbaum, "Objectification," p. 303.

53. Gardner Fair uses the phrase "oddly anachronistic" in describing some of Nussbaum's work on sexuality. See his "Review of *Sex and Social Justice*," *Social Theory and Practice* 25, no. 2 (1999): 350.

54. Nussbaum, "Objectification," p. 310.

55. See Kipnis, "(Male) Desire and (Female) Disgust," p. 380: "[O]bscene jokes and pornographic images *are* perceived by *some* women as an act of aggression against women. But these images and jokes are aggressive only insofar as they're capable of causing the woman discomfort, and they're capable of causing discomfort *only* insofar as there *are* differing levels of sexual inhibition between at least some men and some women."

56. Nussbaum, "Objectification," p. 320 n. 59.

57. Ibid., p. 309.

58. Ibid., p. 308.

59. John Finnis and Martha C. Nussbaum, "Is Homosexual Conduct Wrong? A Philosophical Exchange," in *The Philosophy of Sex: Contemporary Readings*, 3rd ed., ed. Alan Soble (Lanham, Md.: Rowman and Littlefield, 1997), pp. 89–94.

60. Nussbaum, "Objectification," p. 311.

61. Ibid., p. 312. Nussbaum's criticism of casual sex is reminiscent of Walter Berns's conservative critique of pornography in "Pornography vs. Democracy: The Case for Censorship," *Public Interest* 22 (winter 1971): 3–24.

62. Scruton, *Sexual Desire*, p. 346. See Nussbaum's critique of this book, "Sex in the Head," *New York Review of Books*, December 18, 1986, pp. 49–52.

63. Catharine A. MacKinnon, *Feminism Unmodified: Discourses on Life and Law* (Cambridge: Harvard University Press, 1987), p. 209. MacKinnon often utilizes this repetitive style to browbeat readers. For example, "In the nineteenth century, men were looking at pornography, writing theology; looking at pornography, writing literature; looking at pornography, writing laws and designing our political institutions" ("Preface," in Jeffrey Moussaieff Masson, *A Dark Science: Women, Sexuality, and Psychiatry in the Nineteenth Century* [New York: Farrar, Straus and Giroux, 1986], pp. xvii–xviii). In the twentieth century, MacKinnon was looking at pornography, writing feminism; looking at pornography, devising laws; looking at pornography, designing political institutions. On her own account, all that looking, if she did it, should have had a corrupting effect—unless she has a special talent, a feminist immaculate conception, one that male consumers of pornography lack, to look but not be tainted. For a similar point about Andrea Dworkin, see Tucker, "Gender, Fucking, and Utopia," p. 8. Think about Catholic censors reading possibly heretical books.

64. Catharine A. MacKinnon, *Only Words* (Cambridge: Harvard University Press, 1993), pp. 22–23; see also Andrea Dworkin and Catharine A. MacKinnon, *Pornography and Civil Rights: A New Day for Women's Equality* (Minneapolis: Organizing Against Pornography, 1988), p. 68.

65. Nussbaum, "Objectification," p. 308. Nussbaum says the same thing in the later version of this essay, in *Sex and Social Justice*, p. 234.

66. Nussbaum, "Objectification," p. 313.

67. Paul R. Abramson and Haruo Hayashi contrast the high level of s/m pornography in Japan with the country's relatively low incidence of rape, in "Pornography in Japan: Cross-Cultural and Theoretical Considerations," in *Pornography and Sexual Aggression*, ed. Neil M. Malamuth and Edward Donnerstein (Orlando, Fla.: Academic Press, 1984), pp. 173–83. See also Maureen Turim, "The Erotic in Asian Cinema," in *Dirty Looks: Women, Pornography,*

Power, ed. Pamela Church Gibson and Roma Gibson (London: BFI Publishing, 1993), pp. 81–89.

68. Nussbaum's essay on prostitution, " 'Whether from Reason or Prejudice': Taking Money for Bodily Services," in *Sex and Social Justice* (New York: Oxford University Press, 1999), pp. 276–98, which rarely uses the word "objectification" and defends prostitution both morally and legally, almost seems to have been written by a different person than the author of "Objectification." In her essay on prostitution, Nussbaum writes, in an apparently liberal moment,

> Is sex without deep personal knowledge always immoral? It seems to me officious and presuming to use own's own experience to give an affirmative answer to this question, given that people have such varied experiences of sexuality. (p. 292)

Even here she exposes her sexual conservativism, for the sexually liberal question would not have included the word "always," but would have shifted the burden of proof onto those who would claim that casual sexual activity is prima facie morally wrong. That is, the liberal would have asked, "Is it *ever* immoral to engage in sex without deep personal knowledge?" In her essay on prostitution, then, as well as abundantly in her essay on objectification, Nussbaum is herself "officious and presuming."

69. Lawrence, *Lady Chatterley's Lover*, p. 193.

70. Jane Gallop, *Feminist Accused of Sexual Harassment* (Durham, N.C.: Duke University Press, 1997), p. 78.

71. MacKinnon, *Only Words*, p. 27. See my *Sexual Investigations*, pp. 247–49, on MacKinnon's romanticism.

72. Andrea Dworkin, *Intercourse* (New York: Free Press, 1987), p. 137. There is a neat agreement between Dworkin's claim that heterosexual intercourse per se is for women a catastrophe, and Pope John Paul II's observation that "[i]t is not excluded that the man may also be an object to be enjoyed, but the woman is always in that position in relation to the man" (Karol Wojtyła [Pope John Paul II], *Love and Responsibility*, trans. H. T. Willetts [New York: Farrar, Straus, Giroux, 1981], p. 221). Who is the sexist patriarch here? Both? Neither?

73. Andrea Dworkin, *Our Blood* (New York: Harper and Row, 1976), p. 13. Women together never have use for a dildo or cucumber?

74. Leo Bersani, "Is the Rectum a Grave?" *October*, no. 43 (winter 1987): 214.

75. Ruth Colker, "Feminism, Sexuality, and Self: A Preliminary Inquiry into the Politics of Authenticity," *Boston University Law Review* 68, no. 1 (1988): 217.

76. Ibid., p. 219; see p. 233, where Colker ties together sex, love, and authenticity.

77. Ibid., p. 230.

78. Aristotle, *Nicomachean Ethics*, trans. Martin Ostwald (Indianapolis: Bobbs-Merrill, 1962), 1156b6, 1156b25. See my *The Structure of Love* (New Haven, Conn.: Yale University Press, 1990), pp. 186–87.

79. Morgan, "Theory and Practice," p. 165 (italics omitted). Women's unpleasurable and undesired sexual activities that West refers to (see note 21, above) are, on Morgan's view, although not on West's, rapes.

80. Morgan, "Theory and Practice," p. 166.

81. Russell, "Introduction," p. 15, italics added.

82. See my "In Defense of Bacon," *Philosophy of the Social Sciences* 25, no. 2 (1995): 192-215; revised version in *A House Built on Sand: Exposing Postmodernist Myths about Science*, ed. Noretta Koertge (New York: Oxford University Press, 1998), pp. 195–215.

83. Andrea Dworkin, *Right-Wing Women* (New York: Perigee, 1983), p. 60.

84. Dworkin, *Intercourse*, pp. 135–36. The message of "The Wife of Bath's Tale" is not that what women want is to be loved and to be made love to by men despite their own age and flabbiness (as in Chesler), but to be an absolute monarch in their relations with men:

> "A woman wants the self-same sovereignty
> Over her husband as over her lover,
> And master him; he must not be above her."

Geoffrey Chaucer, *The Canterbury Tales*, rev. ed., trans. Nevill Coghill (Baltimore: Penguin Books, 1961), p. 302; see p. 307. Women may *want* "female-first intercourse," but the Wife of Bath never asserts, unlike Woodhull, that they have a natural right to it.

85. Victoria Woodhull, "Tried As By Fire," in *The Victoria Woodhull Reader*, ed. Madeleine B. Stern (Weston, Mass.: M & S Press, 1974), p. 40.

86. Dworkin, *Intercourse*, p. 136.

87. Woodhull, "Tried As By Fire," pp. 26, 30, 37, 43; "The Principles of Social Freedom," in *The Victoria Woodhull Reader*, ed. Madeleine B. Stern (Weston, Mass.: M & S Press, 1974), p. 36.

88. Margaret Jean Intons-Peterson and Beverly Roskos-Ewoldsen, "Mitigating the Effects of Violent Pornography," in *For Adult Users Only: The Dilemma of Violent Pornography*, ed. Susan Gubar and Joan Hoff (Bloomington: Indiana University Press, 1989), p. 219.

89. Lawrence, *Lady Chatterley's Lover*, p. 237.

CONCLUSION
SWEET DREAMS

If all men and women respected each other, if sex were considered joyful and life-enhancing instead of a wallow in germ-filled glop, if everyone were in love all the time, if, in other words, many people's lives were more satisfactory for them than they appear to be now, pornography might just go away on its own.

Margaret Atwood[1]

In my discussion of the feminist and conservative critique of pornography, I have made a number of points. (1) Feminist and conservative moral critiques of pornography frequently rest on illusions about the value of human beings and therefore on platitudinous and unsupportable claims about the wrongness of degradation and dehumanization. (2) Feminist critics of pornography, in purporting to find degradation in its images, buy into—uncritically accept—traditional social standards of what is sexually degrading to the human person. How they read pornography is determined by dominant social meanings, which they in effect endorse (as do the conservative critics of pornography) instead of condemning or transcending. (3) Feminist and conservative critics of pornography do not know much about the genre they criticize. (Much the same can be said about feminist critics of science.) Imagine someone criticizing women's romance novels on the basis of having read a half-dozen books and having examined a score of glossy covers. Such a critique would be unbelievable from the get-go, and its poor empirical foundation would suggest that purely political motives underlie the critique instead of reasoned, objective argument. Feminist and conservative critics of pornography emphasize the worst examples of the genre, trying to get political advantage out of their exaggerations. (4) Feminist and conservative critics of pornography read pornographic images literally, as if engaged in a fundamentalist reading of Genesis. They lack the imagination or the sympathy to read the images in multiple and flexible ways, to try to see them from the various perspectives of their viewers. They promulgate the worst possible readings, and try to get polemical mileage out of their exaggerations. (5) The innocence with which feminist and conservative critics of pornography read pornographic images is matched by their sexual naïveté— which in part explains their reluctance or inability to find multiple meanings in pornographic images. They discuss and pass judgment on sexual practices as if in this domain of human behavior they have as little experience and knowledge as they do of pornographic images. (6) Feminist and conservative critics of pornography assume that sexual relations are ideally, or should only be, carried out in a context of trust, love, commitment, intimacy, mutual respect, and so forth; they are united in their opposition to cold or casual sex. This tendency exhibits the critics' sexual naïveté, their debt to traditional social values and moral illusions, and their prejudice against nonfeminine forms of sexuality. (7) Feminist critics of pornography and patriarchal sexuality pretend to be able to read the minds of men. The inability or unwillingness to understand pornographic images in multiple ways may be a cause or an effect of their inability or unwillingness to read the minds of men more sympathetically, or with more empirical foundation. And (8), feminist and conservative critics of pornography do not do justice to the social and psychological research about pornography and its purported harms, and they use their unwarranted readings of this scientific material, as they use their oversimplified readings of pornography itself, to manufacture their case against pornography and its consumers.

I would be pleased, sometime, to come across a substantial feminist critique of pornography that avoids these problems. Why am I doubtful that such a critique would ever be forthcoming? Perhaps because, using inductive methods, the appearance of this critique, given what we have experienced so far in the writings of feminists on pornography, it is as unlikely as the sun's rising in the west tomorrow. Unlike Atwood, I do not have any sweet dreams about the disappearance of pornography in some beautiful social future; nor do I have any about the eventual success of the feminist critique of pornography. An interesting question is whether the unlikeliness of such a critique is due to the nature of feminist philosophy, to the nature of its scholarly practitioners, or to the nature of the pornography and men's sexuality that they condemn.

NOTE

1. "Atwood on Pornography," *Chatelaine* 56, no. 9 (September 1983): 126.

BIBLIOGRAPHY

Abramson, Paul R., and Haruo Hayashi. "Pornography in Japan: Cross-Cultural and Theoretical Considerations." In *Pornography and Sexual Aggression*, edited by Neil M. Malamuth and Edward Donnerstein, pp. 173–83. Orlando, Fla.: Academic Press, 1984.

Abramson, Paul R., and Steven D. Pinkerton, eds. *Sexual Nature Sexual Culture*. Chicago: University of Chicago Press, 1995.

"American Booksellers Ass'n Inc. v. Hudnut, 771 F.2d 323 (1985)." In *In Harm's Way: The Pornography Civil Rights Hearings*, edited by Catharine A. MacKinnon and Andrea Dworkin, pp. 465–82. Cambridge: Harvard University Press, 1997.

Ariès, Philippe, and André Béjin, eds. *Western Sexuality: Practice and Precept in Past and Present Times*. Oxford: Blackwell, 1985.

Aristotle. *Nicomachean Ethics*. Translated by Martin Ostwald. Indianapolis: Bobbs-Merrill, 1962.

Assiter, Alison, and Avedon Carol, eds. *Bad Girls and Dirty Pictures: The Challenge to Reclaim Feminism*. London: Pluto Press, 1993.

Atwood, Margaret. "Atwood on Pornography." *Chatelaine* 56, no. 9 (September 1983): 61, 118, 126.

Badhwar, Neera Kapur, ed. *Friendship: A Philosophical Reader*. Ithaca, N.Y.: Cornell University Press, 1993.

Baird, Robert M., and Stuart E. Rosenbaum, eds. *Pornography: Private Right or Public Menace?* Rev. ed. Amherst, N.Y.: Prometheus Books, 1998.

Baldwin, Margaret. "The Sexuality of Inequality: The Minneapolis Pornography Ordinance." *Law and Inequality: A Journal of Theory and Practice* 2, no. 2 (1984): 629–53.

Barkey, Jeanne, and J. Koplin. "'Entertainment' for Men: What It Is and What It Means." In *Pornography: Women, Violence and Civil Liberties*, edited by Catherine Itzin, pp. 27–53. Oxford: Oxford University Press, 1992.

Barrowclough, Susan. "Review of 'Not a Love Story,'" *Screen* 23, no. 5 (1982): 26–36.

Bart, Pauline. "Testimony in the Los Angeles Hearing (1985)." In *In Harm's Way: The Pornography Civil Rights Hearings*, edited by Catharine A. MacKinnon and Andrea Dworkin, pp. 342–44. Cambridge: Harvard University Press, 1997.

Berger, Fred R. "Pornography, Sex, and Censorship." In *The Philosophy of Sex*, 1st ed., edited by Alan Soble, pp. 322–47. Totowa, N.J.: Rowman and Littlefield, 1980.

Berns, Walter. "Pornography vs. Democracy: The Case for Censorship." *Public Interest* 22 (winter 1971): 3–24.

Bersani, Leo. *The Freudian Body: Psychoanalysis and Art*. New York: Columbia University Press, 1986.

———. "Is the Rectum a Grave?" *October*, no. 43 (winter 1987): 197–222.

Bishop, Sharon, and Marjorie Weinzweig, eds. *Philosophy and Women*. Belmont, Calif.: Wadsworth, 1979.

Bullough, Vern L., and Bonnie Bullough, eds. *Human Sexuality: An Encyclopedia*. New York: Garland Publishing, 1994.

Burger, John R. *One-Handed Histories: The Eroto-Politics of Gay Male Video Pornography*. New York: Haworth Press, 1995.

Burgess, Ann Wolbert, ed. *Rape and Sexual Assault: A Research Handbook*. New York: Garland, 1985.

Burstyn, Varda, ed. *Women Against Censorship*. Vancouver, B.C.: Douglas and McIntyre, 1985.

Calhoun, Cheshire. "Review of Alan Soble, *Sexual Investigations*." *Ethics* 109, no. 4 (1999): 928–31.

Califia, Pat. "Feminism and Sadomasochism." In *Feminism and Sexuality: A Reader*, edited by Stevi Jackson and Sue Scott, pp. 230–37. New York: Columbia University Press, 1996.

————. *Macho Sluts*. Los Angeles: Alyson Books, 1988.

Carol, Avedon, and Nettie Pollard. "Changing Perceptions in the Feminist Debate." In *Bad Girls and Dirty Pictures: The Challenge to Reclaim Feminism*, edited by Alison Assiter and Avedon Carol, pp. 45–56. London: Pluto Press, 1993.

Carse, Alisa L. "Pornography: An Uncivil Liberty?" *Hypatia* 10, no. 1 (1995): 156–82.

Chaucer, Geoffrey. *The Canterbury Tales*. Translated by Nevill Coghill. Rev. ed. Baltimore: Penguin Books, 1961.

Check, James V. P. "The Effects of Violent Pornography, Nonviolent Dehumanizing Pornography, and Erotica: Some Legal Implications from a Canadian Perspective." In *Pornography: Women, Violence and Civil Liberties*, edited by Catherine Itzin, pp. 350–58. Oxford: Oxford University Press, 1992.

Check, James V. P., and Ted H. Guloien. "Reported Proclivity for Coercive Sex Following Repeated Exposure to Sexually Violent Pornography, Nonviolent Dehumanizing Pornography, and Erotica." In *Pornography: Research Advances and Policy Considerations*, edited by Dolf Zillmann and Jennings Bryant, pp. 159–84. Hillsdale, N.J.: Lawrence Erlbaum, 1989.

Chesler, Phyllis. "Letter, December 7, 1983 (Exhibit 13 [44] in The Minneapolis Hearings)." In *In Harm's Way: The Pornography Civil Rights Hearings*, edited by Catharine A. MacKinnon and Andrea Dworkin, p. 228. Cambridge: Harvard University Press, 1997.

————. "Men and Pornography: Why They Use It." In *Take Back the Night: Women on Pornography*, edited by Laura Lederer, pp. 155–58. New York: William Morrow, 1980.

————. "Opening Statement," in "Panel Discussion: Effects of Violent Pornography." *New York University Review of Law and Social Change* 8, no. 2 (1978–79): 230–32.

Christensen, Ferrel M. "Cultural and Ideological Bias in Pornography Research." *Philosophy of the Social Sciences* 20, no. 3 (1990): 351–75.

Cohen, Joshua. "Freedom, Equality, Pornography." In *Justice and Injustice in Law and Legal Theory*, edited by Austin Sarat and Thomas R. Kearns, pp. 99–137. Ann Arbor: University of Michigan Press, 1996.

Coleman, Julie. *Love, Sex, and Marriage: A Historical Thesaurus.* Amsterdam: Editions Rodopi, 1999.

Colker, Ruth. "Feminism, Sexuality, and Self: A Preliminary Inquiry into the Politics of Authenticity." *Boston University Law Review* 68, no. 1 (1988): 217–64.

Collins, Louise. "Emotional Adultery: Cybersex and Commitment." *Social Theory and Practice* 25, no. 2 (1999): 243–70.

Colter, Ephen Glenn, Wayne Hoffman, Eva Pendleton, Alison Redick, and David Serlin, eds. *Policing Public Sex: Queer Politics and the Future of AIDS Activism.* Boston: South End Press, 1996.

Cornell, Drucilla. "Pornography's Temptation." In *Feminism and Pornography*, edited by Drucilla Cornell, pp. 551–68. Oxford: Oxford University Press, 2000.

———, ed. *Feminism and Pornography.* Oxford: Oxford University Press, 2000.

Cornog, Martha. "Language and Sex." In *Human Sexuality: An Encyclopedia*, edited by Vern L. Bullough and Bonnie Bullough, pp. 341–47. New York: Garland Publishing, 1994.

———. "Sexual Body Parts: Preliminary Patterns and Implications." *Journal of Sex Research* 22, no. 3 (1986): 393–98.

———. "Tom, Dick and Hairy: Notes on Genital Pet Names." *Maledicta* 5, no. 1&2 (1981): 31–40.

Cowie, Elizabeth. "Pornography and Fantasy: Psychoanalytic Perspectives." In *Sex Exposed: Sexuality and the Pornography Debate*, edited by Lynne Segal and Mary McIntosh, pp. 132–52. New Brunswick, N.J.: Rutgers University Press, 1993.

Crispin, Edmund. *The Moving Toyshop.* New York: Penguin Books, 1958.

de Waal, Frans B. M. "Sex as an Alternative to Aggression in the Bonobo." In *Sexual Nature Sexual Culture*, edited by Paul Abramson and Steven Pinkerton, pp. 37–56. Chicago: University of Chicago Press, 1995.

Diamond, Sara. "Pornography: Image and Reality." In *Women Against Censorship*, edited by Varda Burstyn, pp. 40–57. Vancouver, B.C.: Douglas and McIntyre, 1985.

Dietz, Park Elliott. "Statement of Park Elliott Dietz." In *Final Report of the Attorney General's Commission on Pornography*, pp. 487–92. Nashville, Tenn.: Rutledge Hill Press, 1986.

Dreger, Alice Domurat. *Hermaphrodites and the Medical Invention of Sex*. Cambridge: Harvard University Press, 1998.

Dworkin, Andrea. *Intercourse*. New York: Free Press, 1987.

———. *Life and Death*. New York: Free Press, 1997.

———. *Our Blood*. New York: Harper and Row, 1976.

———. *Pornography: Men Possessing Women*. New York: Perigee, 1981.

———. *Right-Wing Women*. New York: Perigee, 1983.

———. "Why So-Called Radical Men Love and Need Pornography." In *Take Back the Night: Women on Pornography*, edited by Laura Lederer, pp. 148–54. New York: William Morrow, 1980.

Dworkin, Andrea, and Catharine A. MacKinnon. *Pornography and Civil Rights: A New Day for Women's Equality*. Minneapolis: Organizing Against Pornography, 1988.

Dwyer, Susan, ed. *The Problem of Pornography*. Belmont, Calif.: Wadsworth, 1995.

Easton, Susan M. *The Problem of Pornography: Regulation and the Right to Free Speech*. London: Routledge, 1994.

Elshtain, Jean Bethke. "The New Porn Wars." *New Republic* (June 25, 1984): 19.

Estlund, David M., and Martha C. Nussbaum, eds. *Sex, Preference, and Family: Essays on Law and Nature*. New York: Oxford University Press, 1997.

Fair, Gardner. "Review of Martha C. Nussbaum's *Sex and Social Justice*." *Social Theory and Practice* 25, no. 2 (1999): 344–52.

Farr, Susan. "The Art of Discipline." In *Coming to Power*, edited by Samois, pp. 181–89. Palo Alto, Calif.: Up Press, 1981.

Final Report of the Attorney General's Commission on Pornography. Nashville, Tenn.: Rutledge Hill Press, 1986.

Finnis, John, and Martha C. Nussbaum. "Is Homosexual Conduct Wrong? A Philosophical Exchange." In *The Philosophy of Sex: Contemporary Readings*, 3rd ed., edited by Alan Soble, pp. 89–94. Lanham, Md.: Rowman and Littlefield, 1997.

Freud, Sigmund. "Fetishism." In *The Standard Edition of the Com-

plete Psychological Works of Sigmund Freud, edited and translated by James Strachey. Vol. 21, pp. 152–57. London: Hogarth Press, 1953–74.

———. *The Future of an Illusion*. In *The Standard Edition of the Complete Psychological Works of Sigmund Freud*, edited and translated by James Strachey. Vol. 21, pp. 5–56. London: Hogarth Press, 1953–74.

———. "On the History of the Psycho-Analytic Movement." in *The Standard Edition of the Complete Psychological Works of Sigmund Freud*, edited and translated by James Strachey. Vol. 14, pp. 7–66. London: Hogarth Press, 1953–74.

———. "On the Universal Tendency to Debasement in the Sphere of Love." In *The Standard Edition of the Complete Psychological Works of Sigmund Freud*, edited and translated by James Strachey. Vol. 11, pp. 179–90. London: Hogarth Press, 1953–74.

———. *Three Essays on the Theory of Sexuality*. In *The Standard Edition of the Complete Psychological Works of Sigmund Freud*, edited and translated by James Strachey. Vol. 7 , pp. 130–243. London: Hogarth Press, 1953–74.

Friend, Tad. "Yes." *Esquire* (February 1994): 48–56.

Gallop, Jane. *Feminist Accused of Sexual Harassment*. Durham, N.C.: Duke University Press, 1997.

Garry, Ann. "Pornography and Respect for Women." In *Philosophy and Women*, edited by Sharon Bishop and Marjorie Weinzweig, pp. 128–39. Belmont, Calif.: Wadsworth, 1979.

Gibson, Pamela Church, and Roma Gibson, eds. *Dirty Looks: Women, Pornography, Power*. London: BFI Publishing, 1993.

Gilbert, Harriet. "So Long as It's Not Sex and Violence: Andrea Dworkin's *Mercy*." In *Sex Exposed: Sexuality and the Pornography Debate*, edited by Lynne Segal and Mary McIntosh, pp. 216–29. New Brunswick, N.J.: Rutgers University Press, 1993.

Gould, Carol C., ed. *Beyond Domination*. Totowa, N.J.: Rowman and Allanheld, 1984.

Griffin, Susan. *Pornography and Silence: Culture's Revenge against Nature*. New York: Harper and Row, 1981.

Grimshaw, Jean. "Ethics, Fantasy and Self-Transformation." In *The*

Philosophy of Sex: Contemporary Readings, 3rd ed., edited by Alan Soble, pp. 175–87. Lanham, Md.: Rowman and Littlefield, 1997.

Grossberg, Lawrence, Cary Nelson, and Paula A. Treichler, eds. *Cultural Studies*. New York: Routledge, 1992.

Gruen, Lori, and George F. Panichas, eds. *Sex, Morality, and the Law*. New York: Routledge, 1997.

Gubar, Susan, and Joan Hoff, eds. *For Adult Users Only: The Dilemma of Violent Pornography*. Bloomington: Indiana University Press, 1989.

Halperin, David M. *Saint Foucault: Towards a Gay Hagiography*. New York: Oxford University Press, 1995.

Hill, Judith M. "Pornography and Degradation." In *Pornography: Private Right or Public Menace?*, rev. ed., edited by Robert M. Baird and Stuart E. Rosenbaum, pp. 100–13. Amherst, N.Y.: Prometheus Books, 1998.

Hite, Shere. *The Hite Report on Male Sexuality*. New York: Alfred A. Knopf, 1981.

Hoffman, Eric. "Feminism, Pornography, and Law." *University of Pennsylvania Law Review* 133, no. 2 (1985): 497–534.

Intons-Peterson, Margaret Jean, and Beverly Roskos-Ewoldsen. "Mitigating the Effects of Violent Pornography." In *For Adult Users Only: The Dilemma of Violent Pornography*, edited by Susan Gubar and Joan Hoff, pp. 218–39. Bloomington: Indiana University Press, 1989.

Itzin, Catherine. "Editor's Introduction" to "District Court of Ontario, *R. v. Ross Wise*, before the Hon. Judge H. R. Locke, 22 June 1990: Reasons for Judgment." In *Pornography: Women, Violence and Civil Liberties*, edited by Catherine Itzin, pp. 603–604. Oxford: Oxford University Press, 1992.

———. "Introduction: Fact, Fiction and Faction." In *Pornography: Women, Violence and Civil Liberties*, edited by Catherine Itzin, pp. 1–24. Oxford: Oxford University Press, 1992.

———, ed. *Pornography: Women, Violence and Civil Liberties*. Oxford: Oxford University Press, 1992.

Jackson, Stevi, and Sue Scott, eds. *Feminism and Sexuality: A Reader*. New York: Columbia University Press, 1996.

Jaggar, Alison M., and Susan R. Bordo, eds. *Gender/Body/Knowledge: Feminist Reconstructions of Being and Knowing*. New Brunswick, N.J.: Rutgers University Press, 1989.

Jarvie, Ian C. "Pornography and/as Degradation." *International Journal of Law and Psychiatry* 14 (1991): 13–27.

———. *Thinking about Society: Theory and Practice*. Dordrecht: D. Reidel, 1986.

Jong, Erica. *Fear of Flying*. New York: Signet, 1973.

Kaite, Berkeley. *Pornography and* Difference. Bloomington: Indiana University Press, 1995.

Kant, Immanuel. *The Metaphysics of Morals*. Translated by Mary Gregor. Cambridge: Cambridge University Press, 1996.

Kappeler, Susanne. *The Pornography of Representation*. Minneapolis: University of Minnesota Press, 1986.

Keller, Evelyn Fox. *A Feeling for the Organism: The Life and Work of Barbara McClintock*. San Francisco: W. H. Freeman, 1983.

Keohane, Nannerl O., Michelle Z. Rosaldo, and Barbara C. Gelpi, eds. *Feminist Theory: A Critique of Ideology*. Chicago: University of Chicago Press, 1982.

Kierkegaard, Søren. *Stages on Life's Way*. Translated by Walter Lowrie. Princeton, N.J.: Princeton University Press, 1945.

———. *Works of Love: Some Christian Reflections in the Form of Discourses*. Translated by Howard and Edna Hong. New York: Harper and Row, 1962.

Kimmel, Michael S. "Introduction: Guilty Pleasures—Pornography in Men's Lives." In *Men Confront Pornography*, edited by Michael S. Kimmel, pp. 1–22. New York: Crown Publishers, 1990.

———, ed. *Men Confront Pornography*. New York: Crown Publishers, 1990.

Kipnis, Laura. *Bound and Gagged: Pornography and the Politics of Fantasy in America*. New York: Grove Press, 1996.

———. "(Male) Desire and (Female) Disgust: Reading *Hustler*." In *Cultural Studies*, edited by Lawrence Grossberg, Cary Nelson, and Paula A. Treichler, pp. 373–91. New York: Routledge, 1992.

Kittay, Eva Feder. "Pornography and the Erotics of Domination."

In *Beyond Domination*, edited by Carol C. Gould, pp. 145–74. Totowa, N.J.: Rowman and Allanheld, 1984.

Kundera, Milan. *The Unbearable Lightness of Being*. New York: Harper and Row, 1984.

Langton, Rae. "Sexual Solipsism." *Philosophical Topics* 23, no. 2 (1995): 149–87.

Laporte, Dominique. *History of Shit*. Translated by Nadia Benabid and Rodolphe el-Khoury. Cambridge: MIT Press, 2000.

Laumann, Edward O., John H. Gagnon, Robert T. Michael, and Stuart Michaels. *The Social Organization of Sexuality: Sexual Practices in the United States*. Chicago: University of Chicago Press, 1994.

Lawrence, D. H. *Lady Chatterley's Lover*. New York: New American Library, 1962.

Lederer, Laura. "'*Playboy* Isn't Playing,' An Interview with Judith Bat-Ada." In *Take Back the Night: Women on Pornography*, edited by Laura Lederer, pp. 121–33. New York: William Morrow, 1980.

———, ed. *Take Back the Night: Women on Pornography*. New York: William Morrow, 1980.

Lederer, Laura, and Diana E. H. Russell. "Questions We Get Asked Most Often." In *Take Back the Night: Women on Pornography*, edited by Laura Lederer, pp. 23–29. New York: William Morrow, 1980.

Lemann, Nicholas. "Southen Discomfort." *New Yorker* (March 13, 2000): 92–96.

Lewin, Ralph A. *Merde: Excursions in Scientific, Cultural, and Sociohistorical Coprology*. New York: Random House, 1999.

Linz, Daniel, and Neil Malamuth. *Pornography*. Newbury Park, Calif.: Sage Publications, 1993.

Longino, Helen E. "Pornography, Oppression, and Freedom: A Closer Look." In *The Problem of Pornography*, edited by Susan Dwyer, pp. 34–47. Belmont, Calif.: Wadsworth, 1995.

MacKinnon, Catharine A. "Feminism, Marxism, Method, and the State: An Agenda for Theory." In *Feminist Theory: A Critique of Ideology*, edited by Nannerl O. Keohane, Michelle Z. Rosaldo, and Barbara C. Gelpi, pp. 1–30. Chicago: University of Chicago Press, 1982.

———. *Feminism Unmodified: Discourses on Life and Law*. Cambridge: Harvard University Press, 1987.

———. *Only Words*. Cambridge: Harvard University Press, 1993.

———. "Pornography Left and Right." In *Sex, Preference, and Family: Essays on Law and Nature*, edited by David M. Estlund and Martha C. Nussbaum, pp. 102–25. New York: Oxford University Press, 1997.

———. "Preface." In Jeffrey Moussaieff Masson, *A Dark Science: Women, Sexuality, and Psychiatry in the Nineteenth Century*, pp. xi–xxii. New York: Farrar, Straus and Giroux, 1986.

———. "Testimony before the Los Angeles Hearing (1985)." In *In Harm's Way: The Pornography Civil Rights Hearings*, edited by Catharine A. MacKinnon and Andrea Dworkin, pp. 332–60. Cambridge: Harvard University Press, 1997.

———. *Toward a Feminist Theory of the State*. Cambridge: Harvard University Press, 1989.

———. "Vindication and Resistance: A Response to the Carnegie Mellon Study of Pornography in Cyberspace." *Georgetown Law Journal* 83 (1995): 1959–67.

MacKinnon, Catharine A., and Andrea Dworkin, eds. *In Harm's Way: The Pornography Civil Rights Hearings*. Cambridge: Harvard University Press, 1997.

Malamuth, Neil M., and Edward Donnerstein, eds. *Pornography and Sexual Aggression*. Orlando, Fla.: Academic Press, 1984.

Manderson, Leonore. "The Pursuit of Pleasure and the Sale of Sex." In *Sexual Nature Sexual Culture*, edited by Paul Abramson and Steven Pinkerton, pp. 305–29. Chicago: University of Chicago Press, 1995.

Mappes, Thomas A., and Jane S. Zembaty, eds. *Social Ethics: Morality and Social Policy*. 5th ed. New York: McGraw-Hill, 1997.

Marietta, Don E., Jr. *Philosophy of Sexuality*. Armonk, N.Y.: M. E. Sharpe, 1997.

Martin, Steve. "Does God Exist?" *New Yorker* (December 7 & 14, 1998): 100–102.

Masson, Jeffrey Moussaieff. *A Dark Science: Women, Sexuality, and*

Psychiatry in the Nineteenth Century. New York: Farrar, Straus and Giroux, 1986.

McClintock, Anne. "Maid to Order: Commercial S/M and Gender Power." In *Dirty Looks: Women, Pornography, Power,* edited by Pamela Church Gibson and Roma Gibson, pp. 207–31. London: BFI Publishing, 1993.

Meilaender, Gilbert. *The Limits of Love: Some Theological Explorations.* University Park: Pennsylvania State University Press, 1987.

Merkin, Daphne. "Sister Act." *New Yorker* (June 14, 1999): 78–84.

Michael, Robert T., John H. Gagnon, Edward O. Laumann, and Gina Kolata. *Sex in America.* Boston: Little, Brown and Company, 1994.

Mill, John Stuart. *On Liberty.* Indianapolis: Hackett, 1978.

Miller, William Ian. *The Anatomy of Disgust.* Cambridge: Harvard University Press, 1997.

Mohr, Richard. *Gay Ideas.* Boston: Beacon Press, 1992.

Morgan, Robin. "Theory and Practice: Pornography and Rape." In *Going Too Far: The Personal Chronicle of a Feminist,* pp. 163–69. New York: Random House, 1977.

Moulton, Janice. "Sexual Behavior: Another Position." In *The Philosophy of Sex: Contemporary Readings,* 3rd ed., edited by Alan Soble, pp. 31–38. Lanham, Md.: Rowman and Littlefield, 1997.

Nagel, Thomas. "Sexual Perversion." In *The Philosophy of Sex: Contemporary Readings,* 3rd ed., edited by Alan Soble, pp. 9–20. Lanham, Md.: Rowman and Littlefield, 1997.

"No-Sex Marriage." *Dallas Morning News,* March 11, 1998, p. 2C.

Nozick, Robert. "Sexuality." In *The Examined Life,* pp. 61–67. New York: Simon and Schuster, 1989.

Nussbaum, Martha C. "Objectification." In *The Philosophy of Sex: Contemporary Readings,* 3rd ed., edited by Alan Soble, pp. 283–321. Lanham, Md.: Rowman and Littlefield, 1997.

———. "Objectification." In *Sex and Social Justice,* pp. 213–39. New York: Oxford University Press, 1999.

———. *Sex and Social Justice.* New York: Oxford University Press, 1999.

———. "Sex in the Head." *New York Review of Books,* December 18, 1986, pp. 49–52.

———. " 'Whether From Reason or Prejudice.' Taking Money for

Bodily Services." In *Sex and Social Justice*, pp. 276–98. New York: Oxford University Press, 1999.

O'Hara, Scott. "Talking with My Mouth Full." In *Policing Public Sex: Queer Politics and the Future of AIDS Activism*, edited by Ephen Glenn Colter, Wayne Hoffman, Eva Pendleton, Alison Redick, and David Serlin, pp. 81–86. Boston: South End Press, 1996.

Olivieri, Achillo. "Eroticism and Social Groups in Sixteenth-Century Venice: The Courtesan." In *Western Sexuality: Practice and Precept in Past and Present Times*, edited by Philippe Ariès and André Béjin, pp. 94–102. Oxford: Blackwell, 1985.

O'Neill, Eileen. "(Re)presentations of Eros: Exploring Female Sexual Agency." In *Gender/Body/Knowledge: Feminist Reconstructions of Being and Knowing*, edited by Alison M. Jaggar and Susan R. Bordo, pp. 68–91. New Brunswick, N.J.: Rutgers University Press, 1989.

O'Neill, Nora. *Constructions of Reason: Explorations of Kant's Practical Philosophy*. Cambridge: Cambridge University Press, 1989.

Overall, Christine. "What's Wrong with Prostitution? Evaluating Sex Work." *Signs* 17, no. 4 (1992): 705–24.

Paglia, Camille. *Sex, Art, and American Culture: Essays*. New York: Vintage Books, 1992.

"Panel Discussion: Effects of Violent Pornography." *New York University Review of Law and Social Change* 8, no. 2 (1978–79): 225–45.

Patai, Daphne. *Heterophobia: Sexual Harassment and the Future of Feminism*. Lanham, Md.: Rowman and Littlefield, 1998.

Pateman, Carole. *The Sexual Contract*. Stanford, Calif.: Stanford University Press, 1988.

Paton, H. J. "Kant on Friendship." In *Friendship: A Philosophical Reader*, edited by Neera Kapur Badhwar, pp. 133–54. Ithaca, N.Y.: Cornell University Press, 1993.

Payer, Pierre J. *The Bridling of Desire: Views of Sex in the Later Middle Ages*. Toronto: University of Toronto Press, 1993.

Penley, Constance. "Crackers and Whackers: The White Trashing of Porn." In *White Trash: Race and Class in America*, edited by

Matt Wray and Annalee Newitz, pp. 89–112. New York: Routledge, 1977.

Plato. *Symposium*. In *Eros, Agape, and Philia: Readings in the Philosophy of Love*, edited by Alan Soble, pp. 46–56. St. Paul, Minn.:
Paragon House, 1989.

Posner, Richard, and Katharine Silbaugh. *A Guide to America's Sex
Laws*. Chicago: University of Chicago Press, 1996.

Punzo, Vincent C. "Morality and Human Sexuality." In *Social
Ethics: Morality and Social Policy*, 5th ed., edited by Thomas A.
Mappes and Jane S. Zembaty, pp. 157–62. New York: McGraw-
Hill, 1997.

Reich, Wilhelm. *The Discovery of the Orgone. Vol. 1: The Function of
the Orgasm*. New York: Noonday Press, 1961.

Rimm, Marty. "Marketing Pornography on the Information Superhighway: A Survey of 917,410 Images, Descriptions, Short Sto-
ries, and Animations Downloaded 8.5 Million Times by Consumers in Over 2000 Cities in Forty Countries, Provinces, and
Territories." *Georgetown Law Journal* 83 (1995): 1849–1934.

Roth, Philip. *Portnoy's Complaint*. New York: Random House, 1969.

Rubin, Gayle. "The Leather Menace: Comments on Politics and
S/M." In *Coming to Power*, edited by Samois, pp. 192–225. Palo
Alto, Calif.: Up Press, 1981.

———. "Misguided, Dangerous and Wrong: An Analysis of Anti-
Pornography Politics." In *Bad Girls and Dirty Pictures: The Chal-
lenge to Reclaim Feminism*, edited by Alison Assiter and Avedon
Carol, pp. 18–40. London: Pluto Press, 1993.

Rubin, Lillian B. *Erotic Wars: What Happened to the Sexual Revolution?* New York: Farrar, Straus and Giroux, 1990.

———. *Intimate Strangers: Men and Women Together*. New York:
Harper and Row, 1983.

———. "Women, Men, and Intimacy." In *Eros, Agape, and Philia:
Readings in the Philosophy of Love*, edited by Alan Soble, pp.
12–28. St. Paul, Minn.: Paragon House, 1989.

Russell, Diana E. H. "Introduction." In *Making Violence Sexy: Feminist Views on Pornography*, edited by Diana E. H. Russell, pp.
1–20. New York: Teachers College Press, 1993.

————. "Pornography and Rape: A Causal Model." *Political Psychology* 9, no. 1 (1988): 41–73.

————. "Pornography and Violence: What Does the New Research Say?" In *Take Back the Night: Women on Pornography*, edited by Laura Lederer, pp. 218–38. New York: William Morrow, 1980.

————, ed. *Making Violence Sexy: Feminist Views on Pornography*. New York: Teachers College Press, 1993.

Sabbath, Dan, and Mandel Hall. *End Product: The First Taboo*. New York: Urizen Books, 1977.

Samois, ed. *Coming to Power*. Palo Alto, Calif.: Up Press, 1981.

Sanders, Stephanie, and June Reinisch. "Would You Say You 'Had Sex' If . . . ?" *Journal of the American Medical Association* 281, no. 3 (January 20, 1999): 275–77.

Sarat, Austin, and Thomas R. Kearns, eds. *Justice and Injustice in Law and Legal Theory*. Ann Arbor: University of Michigan Press, 1996.

Schopenhauer, Arthur. *The World as Will and Representation*. Vol. 2. Translated by E. F. J. Payne. Indian Hills, Colo.: Falcon's Wing Press, 1958.

Scruton, Roger. *Sexual Desire: A Moral Philosophy of the Erotic*. New York: Free Press, 1986.

Searle, Judith. "Penis Envy." *Cosmopolitan* (June 1975): 189.

Segal, Lynne. "Does Pornography Cause Violence? The Search for Evidence." In *Dirty Looks: Women, Pornography, Power*, edited by Pamela Church Gibson and Roma Gibson, pp. 5–21. London: BFI Publishing, 1993.

Segal, Lynne, and Mary McIntosh, eds. *Sex Exposed: Sexuality and the Pornography Debate*. New Brunswick, N.J.: Rutgers University Press, 1993.

Senn, Charlene Y. "The Research on Women and Pornography: The Many Faces of Harm." In *Making Violence Sexy: Feminist Views on Pornography*, edited by Diana E. H. Russell, pp. 179–93. New York: Teachers College Press, 1993.

Sherfey, Mary Jane. *The Nature and Evolution of Female Sexuality*. New York: Vintage, 1973.

Shrage, Laurie. "Is Sexual Desire Raced?: The Social Meaning of

Interracial Prostitution." *Journal of Social Philosophy* 23, no. 1 (1992): 42–51.

Small, Meredith F. "Prime Mates: The Useful Promiscuity of Bonobo Apes." *Nerve.* Available online at www.nerve.com/small/bonobo/bonobo.html.

Soble, Alan. "Bad Apples: Feminist Politics and Feminist Scholarship." *Philosophy of the Social Sciences* 29, no. 3 (1999): 354–88.

———. "In Defense of Bacon." *Philosophy of the Social Sciences* 25, no. 2 (1995): 192–215. Revised version in *A House Built on Sand: Exposing Postmodernist Myths about Science*, edited by Noretta Koertge, pp. 195–215 (New York: Oxford University Press, 1998).

———. *The Philosophy of Sex and Love: An Introduction.* St. Paul, Minn.: Paragon House, 1998.

———. "Pornography and the Social Sciences." *Social Epistemology* 2, no. 2 (1988): 135–44.

———. "Pornography: Defamation and the Endorsement of Degradation." *Social Theory and Practice* 11, no. 1 (1985): 61–87.

———. *Pornography: Marxism, Feminism, and the Future of Sexuality.* New Haven, Conn.: Yale University Press, 1986.

———. "Review of Susanne Kappeler's *The Pornography of Representation.*" *Philosophy of the Social Sciences* 19, no. 1 (1989): 128–31.

———. *Sexual Investigations.* New York: New York University Press, 1996.

———. "Sexual Use and What to Do about It: Internalist and Externalist Sexual Ethics." *Essays in Philosophy* 2, no. 2 (2001). Available online at www.humboldt.edu/~essays/soble.htm. Revised version in *The Philosophy of Sex: Contemporary Readings*, 4th ed., edited by Alan Soble (Lanham, Md.: Rowman and Littlefield, 2002); available online at www.uno.edu/~asoble/pages/essays.htm.

———. *The Structure of Love.* New Haven, Conn.: Yale University Press, 1990.

———, ed. *Eros, Agape, and Philia: Readings in the Philosophy of Love.* St. Paul, Minn.: Paragon House, 1989.

———. *The Philosophy of Sex: Contemporary Readings.* 1st ed. Totowa, N.J.: Rowman and Littlefield, 1980.

————. *The Philosophy of Sex: Contemporary Readings.* 3rd ed. Lanham, Md.: Rowman and Littlefield, 1997.

————. *The Philosophy of Sex: Contemporary Readings.* 4th ed. Lanham, Md.: Rowman and Littlefield, 2002.

Specter, Michael. "The Dangerous Philosopher." *New Yorker* (September 6, 1999): 46–55.

Stark, Cynthia A. "Is Pornography an Action?: The Causal vs. the Conceptual View of Pornography's Harm." *Social Theory and Practice* 23, no. 2 (1997): 277–306.

Stern, Madeleine B., ed. *The Victoria Woodhull Reader.* Weston, Mass.: M & S Press, 1974.

Stoltenberg, John. *Refusing To Be a Man: Essays on Sex and Justice.* Portland, Ore.: Breitenbush Books, 1989.

Strossen, Nadine. *Defending Pornography: Free Speech, Sex, and the Fight for Women's Rights.* New York: Scribner, 1995.

Tisdale, Sallie. "Talk Dirty to Me." In *The Philosophy of Sex*, 3rd ed., edited by Alan Soble, pp. 271–81. Lanham, Md.: Rowman and Littlefield, 1997.

Tucker, Scott. "Gender, Fucking, and Utopia." *Social Text* #27 (1990): 3–34.

Turim, Maureen. "The Erotic in Asian Cinema." In *Dirty Looks: Women, Pornography, Power*, edited by Pamela Church Gibson and Roma Gibson, pp. 81–89. London: BFI Publishing, 1993.

Vadas, Melinda. "The Pornography/Civil Rights Ordinance v. The BOG: And the Winner Is. . .?" *Hypatia* 7, no. 3 (1992): 94–109.

Vance, Carole S. "Negotiating Sex and Gender in the Attorney General's Commission on Pornography." In *Sex Exposed: Sexuality and the Pornography Debate*, edited by Lynne Segal and Mary McIntosh, pp. 29–49. New Brunswick, N.J.: Rutgers University Press, 1993.

Vannoy, Russell. *Sex Without Love: A Philosophical Exploration.* Amherst, N.Y.: Prometheus Books, 1980.

Voltaire. *Candide.* Translated by Lowell Bair. New York: Bantam Books, 1959.

Weaver, James. "The Social Science and Psychological Research Evidence: Perceptual and Behavioural Consequences of Exposure to Pornography." In *Pornography: Women, Violence and Civil Liberties*, edited by Catherine Itzin, pp. 284–309. Oxford: Oxford University Press, 1992.

Weinberg, Thomas S., ed. *S & M: Studies in Dominance and Submission*. Amherst, N.Y.: Prometheus Books, 1995.

West, Robin. "The Harms of Consensual Sex." In *The Philosophy of Sex: Contemporary Readings*, 3rd ed., edited by Alan Soble, pp. 263–68. Lanham, Md.: Rowman and Littlefield, 1997.

Wheeler, Hollis. "Pornography and Rape: A Feminist Perspective." In *Rape and Sexual Assault: A Research Handbook*, edited by Ann Wolbert Burgess, pp. 374–91. New York: Garland, 1985.

Williams, Linda. *Hard Core: Power, Pleasure, and the "Frenzy of the Visible."* Berkeley: University of California Press, 1989.

———. "A Provoking Agent: The Pornography and Performance Art of Annie Sprinkle." In *Dirty Looks: Women, Pornography, Power*, edited by Pamela Church Gibson and Roma Gibson, pp. 176–91. London: BFI Publishing, 1993.

———. "Second Thoughts on *Hard Core*: American Obscenity Law and the Scapegoating of Deviance." In *Dirty Looks: Women, Pornography, Power*, edited by Pamela Church Gibson and Roma Gibson, pp. 46–61. London: BFI Publishing, 1993.

———. "Sexual Politics: Strange Bedfellows." *In These Times* (October 29–November 4, 1986): 18–20.

Wojtyła, Karol [Pope John Paul II]. *Love and Responsibility*. Translated by H. T. Willetts. New York: Farrar, Straus, Giroux, 1981.

Wolf, Naomi. *The Beauty Myth: How Images of Beauty Are Used Against Women*. New York: Doubleday, 1992.

Woodhull, Victoria. "The Principles of Social Freedom." In *The Victoria Woodhull Reader*, edited by Madeleine B. Stern. Weston, Mass.: M & S Press, 1974.

———. "Tried As By Fire." In *The Victoria Woodhull Reader*, edited by Madeleine B. Stern. Weston, Mass.: M & S Press, 1974.

Wray, Matt, and Annalee Newitz, eds. *White Trash: Race and Class in America*. New York: Routledge, 1977.

Yeats, William Butler. *The Collected Poems of W. B. Yeats*. Edited by Richard J. Finneran. New York: Macmillan, 1989.

Zeitoun, Mary-Lou. "Sexist Piggery Has Women's Section." *Globe and Mail* (Toronto), November 10, 1997, p. A14.

Zillmann, Dolf. *Connections between Sex and Aggression.* Hillsdale, N.J.: Lawrence Erlbaum, 1984.

Zillmann, Dolf, and Jennings Bryant. "Effects of Massive Exposure to Pornography." In *Pornography and Sexual Aggression*, edited by Neil M. Malamuth and Edward Donnerstein, pp. 115–38. Orlando, Fla.: Academic Press, 1984.

———. "Pornography, Sexual Callousness, and the Trivialization of Rape." *Journal of Communication* 32, no. 4 (1982): 10–21.

———. "Pornography's Impact on Sexual Satisfaction." *Journal of Applied Social Psychology* 18, no. 5 (1988): 438–53.

———, eds. *Pornography: Research Advances and Policy Considerations.* Hillsdale, N.J.: Lawrence Erlbaum, 1989.

INDEX

Abramson, Paul
  on rape and pornography in Japan, 190 n. 67
Adam
  objectification of animals, 75
Adam and Eve, 84 n. 40, 126
adultery, 126, 149, 185 n. 19
agape, 79 n. 8, 104
Agathon, 168
American Philosophical Association, 168, 172
anal fingering, 70–71, 138 n. 60
anal intercourse, 112, 115–20, 124, 138 n. 54, 138 n. 55, 138 n. 60, 174
  in pornography, 22, 123, 178
anal yoga, 136 n. 44
anilingis, 120–22, 138 n. 60, 146
anticipation of sex, 38
anus, 51, 91, 113, 115, 120, 121, 137 n. 48
  female, 22, 28, 49, 95, 102, 114, 115, 119
  male, 25, 70–71, 115
Aquinas, Saint Thomas
  on bestiality, 68, 85 n. 50
  natural law, 119

Aretino
  on power of buttocks, 49, 50
Asian(s)
  in pornography, 20, 25, 134 n. 33, 172–73, 190 n. 67
  prostitutes, 128–29
Atwood, Margaret
  sweet dreams about pornography, 195, 197
Augustine, Saint (Bishop of Hippo)
  on the nature of sexuality, 65, 84 n. 40, 97, 121
  original sin, 79 n. 8
  role of God's grace, 68
  sexual desire and slavery, 182
authentic sexuality, 175–76
autonomy, 81 n. 23, 117
  loss of in sex, 66, 164
  retained in sex, 182

Baldwin, Margaret, 23
  on sexual equality in pornography, 14, 159
  on violent pornography, 13–14
Barkey, Jeanne
  defends *Final Report of the Attor-*